Bread of the World

Bread of the World

Christ and the Eucharist Today

John Hadley

Foreword by Bishop Trevor Huddleston

Darton, Longman and Todd
London

First published in 1989 by
Darton, Longman and Todd Ltd
89 Lillie Road, London SW6 1UD

© 1989 John Hadley

British Library Cataloguing in Publication Data

Hadley, John
  Bread of the world.
  1. Christian church. Eucharist
  I. Title
  264′.36

  ISBN 0–232–51837–8

Phototypeset by Input Typesetting Ltd, London SW19 8DR
Printed and bound in Great Britain by
Courier International Ltd
Tiptree, Essex

Contents

Foreword

Almost every day I walk past a famous booksellers in the heart of London's West End. Considerable care is taken to use the windows as a show-case for the latest books and to display them with professional skill. And, always, the shop itself is full of customers in every section, and this in spite of the fact that prices soar – even for paperbacks.

Although the display of religious books is comparatively small it, too, has a constant flow of new titles: an indication, certainly, that the public has still a considerable interest in the subject and a readiness to spend money on it. If this is true of a prestigious bookseller catering for every taste it is certainly also true of those who sell only theological books and of the publishers and their authors who produce them. Yet, we are told, the real problem is that the number of books on the market is so vast and the competition for sales is so intense that the life of a new book is far shorter than it was a decade or so ago and it has to be a book of quite exceptional value or a publisher of special wisdom and judgement which will make it 'notable' or even noticeable to the reading public. Of course, once an author – in whatever field he writes – has achieved eminence in that field and becomes a household name there is no problem. Bishop John Robinson had written a number of excellent theological works (and had become a bishop on the strength of his scholarship) long before *Honest to God* broke upon the church and, in a true sense, changed it. But there have been other such books which have had the same effect over the years from a much quieter birth. I can think of several in my own lifetime and within the context of theology or spirituality which have had (and still have) a profound effect on the very development of Christian thinking. For example, Michael Ramsey's *The Gospel and the Catholic Church*, written when he was still a lecturer at Lincoln Theological College, is a seminal book – perhaps his greatest original contribution to theological debate in this half-century.

Which brings me, at last, to the present book *Bread of the World,* subtitled 'Christ and the Eucharist Today', by John Hadley.

It is very easy to use clichés or bland expressions of pleasure when asked to write a Foreword to *any* book. But if I did so in the present case I would not be able to forgive myself. I had the great privilege and responsibility of ordaining him when I was Bishop of Stepney some fifteen years ago and of observing him in his first curacy. I knew then what considerable intellectual and academic distinction he brought to the ministry and I also knew that he was a young priest exceptionally graced to communicate the truth of the Gospel by his preaching and by his pastoral gifts. And all of this sustained by a spirituality which was unobtrusive and disciplined but never destroyed of 'busy-ness'.

So, I can say with truth, it is an honour to be invited to commend this, his first book. And I will go further and dare to utter a word of prophecy. It is only a beginning of greater things to come.

I have read every word and found myself enthralled by the quality of the writing and the scholarship which lies behind it. Again, a scholarship which is unobtrusive but profound – the kind of scholarship which was recognized by a first in English at Oxford but which is so vastly removed from a purely academic discipline. John Hadley has learnt not from books but from experience as a parish priest and, now, as a university chaplain. I will not spoil the reader's pleasure by quoting at length from the book itself. It must, in any case, be read as a whole because as John Hadley himself says, 'The Eucharist shows us heaven "in ordinary" and the world, and our humanity, glorious in the clear light of heaven.' Every chapter, every paragraph even, deepens our understanding of this marvellous theme.

Yet it is (like each of the gospels) a very short book. For this reason it is *available* to all kinds of readers. To students – whether of theology or of humanity itself: to clergy of any 'school of thought', of every age: to the great family of the catholic church – that is to say, the universal church across nationalities and cultures and historical divides: to those whose interest in 'religion' is superficial or even hostile and to those across religious divisions in our global village, God's world.

I hope and pray that this book will be the bestseller it deserves to be and I am sure that it will be blest by God and a blessing to all who read it.

THE RT. REVD. TREVOR HUDDLESTON CR

Acknowledgements

The scriptural quotations are taken from the Revised Standard Version of the Bible, copyrighted 1971 and 1952 by the Division of Christian Education of the National Council of the Churches of Christ in the USA.

Introduction

Church is boring. To be religious is a mildly pitiable defect, like
flat-footedness or dyslexia: understandable in the old and
neurotic, maybe good for children too, but irrelevant for
normal people and everyday life. That is probably most
people's view, if they have a view; and the Church has helped
foster it, with services that are either dreary, or other-worldly,
or both.

Yet proper Christianity encourages us, not to escape from
the world, but to engage with it in all its unspeakable richness,
as Jesus did; and the Eucharist, at the heart of Christian
worship, expresses this engagement. The bread we offer and
receive is the bread of the *world*; the Christ we celebrate is
not up in the clouds or away in the past, but here, now, in
ordinary material things – feelings, words, people, food and
drink. The Eucharist shows us heaven 'in ordinary', and the
world, and our humanity, glorious in the clear light of heaven.

The Eucharist is a source of excitement and wonder. In
my fifteen years as a priest I must have 'celebrated' thousands
of times, and there have always been, beyond the inevitable
drynesses, new insights and new challenges waiting; and there
always will be. The idea of this book is to share some of these
riches: to take that framework for worship which we call the
Liturgy, slow it down, look at it section by section, and see
what lies hidden there.

One of the discoveries I have made (like most discoveries,
it's been found before, but perhaps never in quite the same
way) is how the shape of the Eucharist mirrors the life of
Christ. The Gospel story is in two main sections: the *revelation*
of God's Kingdom, through the life and teaching of Jesus
(centred on Galilee); and the *offering* of that life to God

(centred on Jerusalem). The Eucharist, similarly, is in two major movements: the *Ministry of the Word*, which communicates the person and teaching of Jesus through readings, sermon, and silence; and the *Thanksgiving*, which catches us up in his sacrifice and commissions us with his life. So, as we move through the drama of the Eucharist, we will relive also the story of Jesus Christ, from the announcement of his coming to his sharing of the Holy Spirit.

But neither the Eucharist, nor the life of Christ which it reveals, are to be separated off from the life of the *world*. Jesus didn't stay aloof from the world's life, in all its glory and ghastliness, but entered it fully, took it on board as it were, and offered it to God. And the Eucharist continues this representative, 'priestly', life of Christ, involving us in it at every level. It is not just our personal shames and troubles, hopes and joys, that we offer to God, but those of our whole world; our Communion does not set us right with God but apart from everyone else, rather it expresses and renews our unity with all people and with the whole created order.

Like a braided loaf, the Eucharist weaves our life together with the life of Christ and the life of the world, interpreting each in the light of the others. We are not just to hear but to *be* the Word of God; we offer not just a distant Jesus, not just an irrelevant wafer, but all humanity for consecration; we not merely receive but *become* the Body of Christ broken, his Blood poured out, for the world.

I hope that, for Christian readers, the book may uncover some fresh meaning in familiar material. Recently the Eucharist has become more central to many churches of the Protestant tradition, and more accessible in the Catholic church: but still there is a tendency to take it on trust, a ritual we go through merely because Jesus ordained it and the Church requires it, an incomprehensible mystery which somehow sets us right with God as long as the priest is validly ordained and says the correct formulae. True mysteries, however, are never just obscure: they can't be fathomed, but they can and should be explored.

As for any non-Christian readers, I hope they will be able

to find some sense and meaning behind this rather heavily Christian framework. I am not concerned here to 'prove' the truth of the gospel story or the traditions of the Church, only to use them to express what makes sense to me. This is not the only spiritual language around, just the only one I can speak with any fluency: so I hope those who normally talk a different language, or a different dialect of this one, can make due allowance; and will forgive me for using 'we', 'us', and 'our' when they don't actually feel included.

In quoting from the Bible, I have used the Revised Standard Version for the Old Testament and my own translations for the New Testament. I have tried to get round the awkward business of the gender of imaginary people by making them alternately male and female.

Finally, my thanks to a lot of people. To the congregations of St Mary and St George, High Wycombe and St Paul, Clifton, to my colleagues in those two places, and to my parents, for their support, encouragement and forbearance during the two years it has taken me to write this book. To the Diocese of Oxford, the Trustees of the Bayne Benefaction, and the British Trustees of the Ecumenical Institute at Tantur, Jerusalem, for financing the sabbatical leave during which I began it: and to Dr Landrum Bolling and the community of that Institute, for the highly stimulating three months I spent there. To the Reverend Mother and Sisters of the Community of St Katharine of Alexandria, Parmoor, where much of the work was done, for understanding my eccentric demands and providing an endless supply of peace and good food. To Celia Deane-Drummond for lending me her word-processor and unveiling its mysteries; to Martin Gainsborough, Leonora Wilson, Dr Robert Ellis and Fr Christopher Burdon for reading through the material, and for the very helpful comments they made. To Bishop Trevor Huddleston for agreeing to write the Foreword; to Lesley Riddle, and everyone at Darton, Longman and Todd, for their help and encouragement; and, last but not least, to my cousin the Rural Dean of Chew Magna for his help with the proofs.

1

Welcome
The Hospitality of God

In the beginning of C. S. Lewis' story of the *Dawn Treader*,
the third of his *Chronicles of Narnia*, the children Edmund,
Lucy and Eustace are together in an upstairs room, looking
at a picture. It is the picture of a ship on a sea, colourful and
exciting; and Edmund and Lucy, who already know some of
the mysteries of the great lion Aslan and his world, immedi-
ately recognize it as a very 'Narnian' picture – for which they
are ruthlessly mocked by the extremely un-Narnian Eustace.
But then, as they look at the picture, it begins to change and
grow; the ship moves; salt spray splashes out on to their faces;
and suddenly there they are, floundering in the Narnian sea,
their ears filled with water and the cries of the seabirds and
of the sailors of the *Dawn Treader*.[1]

There are two ways of seeing a picture, a subject: from
outside, cool, safe, detached; or, like Lewis' children, from
within, caught up, captivated and risking change. So we can
look at God, too, from outside, think about him coolly,
worship from afar; and many religions encourage this, for
what could we have in common with God? But the God of
Christian experience will not stay aloof or let us alone: he
invites us into his very being, splashes out water all over us,
engulfs us in the sea of his love.

Our God is a hospitable God; that is our Good News. We
acclaim Jesus as God's Son, but he was never jealous of that
special relationship; his whole purpose was to share it. At the
beginning of his Gospel, John paints what might seem a very
distant picture of God:

> In the beginning was the Word,
> and the Word was towards God,
> and the Word was God . . .[2]

But this, too, is a Narnian picture, inviting us in:

> As many as received him,
> (those with faith in his name)
> he gave them power to become children of God.[3]

And soon the divine hospitality comes down to earth in the story of Jesus:

> Jesus saw them following him,
> and said to them, 'What are you looking for?'
> They said to him, 'Rabbi, where are you staying?'
> He said to them, 'Come, and you will see.'
> So they came, and saw where he was staying,
> and stayed with him that day.[4]

The story of Jesus is full of such images: meals and banquets are often the subject of his stories, or the setting in which he tells them; his whole life is a parable of divine generosity, an invitation to share his Christhood.

The theme runs through the New Testament. Paul pictures God's people as a body,[5] John as a vine,[6] Peter as a temple:[7] but all reflect this same radical, outrageous Gospel: we aren't called to be just admirers or followers or even friends of the Christ; but literally to be *christened* ourselves – to be baptized with his own baptism, to drink his own cup, to be built into his very being; to enjoy with him the life of the Trinity, to be divinized in our turn as the sons and daughters of God.

It is not surprising, then, that the longest established Christian pictures – icons – have about them this same hospitable, 'Narnian' quality of drawing us into the mystery of God. An icon, painted with love and deep prayer, is never a mere object for study or admiration, but an invitation to set foot in the Kingdom, now. This is partly achieved by the technique of 'reverse perspective', the apparent lack of proportion giving an almost holographic effect; while the most important and marvellous icons are often so dark and worn that the faces can hardly be seen – but here, too, is an invitation, for we also belong there: like those gaudy scenes at fairgrounds where you put your head through a hole and get photographed as a Spanish dancer or Al Capone, it awaits our faces for its completion.

This is particularly true of icons of the Trinity, which is traditionally portrayed in two ways. First, there are the pictures of Christ's *baptism*. Here is Jesus in the waters of the Jordan, being baptized by John; and, as our eyes adjust to the darkish light of Christian tradition, we can see, beyond the merely human encounter, the radiance in the skies, the hand of the Father, the Dove descending; we can imagine the voice from heaven: 'This is my beloved Son!' But there is more: in many such icons Jesus is not alone in the waters; he is in there with a man and a woman. Who are these? As we ask and look, it is once again as if the picture were growing larger, the water splashing out over our faces, and we in our turn were there in the river, *in Christ*; we too feel the breath of the Spirit and the fullness of humanity; we too are acclaimed as the beloved children of God.

The other image of the Trinity is that of the 'Mystical Supper', the story in Genesis of the Three Men who visited Abraham and Sarah under the Oak of Mamre.[8] This picture, of which Rublev's great icon is the best-known example, ostensibly shows the 'hospitality of Abraham'; in fact it looks far more as if the Three Men are offering hospitality to us – the table is spread, they are sitting round the further three sides of it, and the 'reverse perspective' of the icon invites us to make a fourth. And in Rublev's picture not only is there some sort of cup or chalice *on* the table, but the angels on either side have themselves formed a chalice: the whole picture, the very being of God, is a cup we are invited to share.

It is no coincidence that these two pictures of the Trinity, one of Christ's baptism, the other of God's banquet, reflect so closely the two major Christian Sacraments: Baptism and the Eucharist. For the Sacraments also invite us to share the life of Christ, to participate in the Godhead: only here we are not limited to looking and imagining, here we are really part of the picture, true actors in the drama. The Sacraments are icons come alive. At Baptism the water actually is splashed over us, we actually are affirmed as the sons and daughters of God; at the Eucharist we really do lay a table for God, then find ourselves bidden to eat and drink at his feast.

The Eucharist is a gateway into the life of Christ. At the Last Supper, Jesus said 'Do this in remembrance of me': but not so that we can magically or mystically project ourselves back into his past, or conjure him into our present; not so that we can pretend we are already up in heaven, or summon him back down to earth. The Eucharist makes real Christ's eternal life, here and now; it is the sign of God's eternal and continuing hospitality. The ancient mosaic of the loaves and fishes by the Sea of Galilee shows only four loaves; the fifth is the living bread on the altar above, continuing the miracle into the present.

This is also made clear in John's account of the Last Supper. He gives no description of the Supper itself, which would probably have been well known to his readers already; but offers instead, in chapters 13–17, an extended meditation on its divine hospitality:

'If I am to go and prepare a place for you,
I am coming again, and I will take you to my side,
so that where I am you too may be.' (14:3)
'In that day you will know that I am in the Father,
and you in me, and I in you.' (14:20)
'If someone loves me, he will cherish my word,
and my Father will love him,
and we will come to him and make a dwelling with him.'
(14:23)
'Everything the Father has is mine;
therefore . . . [the Spirit] . . . takes from what is mine,
and declares it to you.' (16:15)
'[May they] all be one,
just as you, Father, are in me, and I in you,
so may they be in us . . .' (17:21)

The Gospel invites us to share the fullness of Christ's life in the Godhead; in the Eucharist that invitation is brought fully home: welcome to the feast. We participate in his life by sharing his Word, then his Body and Blood – and also by reliving his life: for in a curious way the Eucharist reflects the pattern of the Gospel story: preparation, teaching, recognition, self-offering, breaking, new life, empowering. So it is fitting that the service should begin with a greeting, a welcome on behalf of the Trinity:

> In the Name of the Father, and of the Son, and of the Holy Spirit:
> the grace of our Lord Jesus Christ,
> and the love of God,
> and the communion of the Holy Spirit, be with you all.[9]

The Eucharist affirms our part in the feast of God's life: although most of the time that life seems impossibly far away. Just occasionally, indeed – in the presence of exceptional godliness; in the light of inspired teaching or reading; when a costly stand is made for God's truth; and when love actually does shine triumphant through our churchy pettinesses – just occasionally it *is* possible to say (though not too loudly) that, through the life of the Church, God's light and breath have broken through into our grubby and humdrum world, that humanity has broken through into heaven and been revealed as divine. But these moments of transfiguration are rare, and do not come to order; most of the time, if we are aware of any divinity in us, it is more likely to be through the pain of unfulfilled longing than through any sense of heavenly consummation.

For our creation is still incomplete. There is an idea, which owes more to Milton than to Genesis, that we somehow started off perfect and then fell catastrophically from grace. But surely, rather, we have started off as children, and are now being gradually drawn out of the sludge towards our true and full humanity, the humanity which Genesis chapter 1 describes as being in the image and likeness of God; so that the Life and the Spirit which God promises are rather a completion of our creation (which is also the work of the Holy Spirit), than merely a reversal of the Fall. We could even say

5

the Fall was a weaning, a necessary part of the redemptive process: we had to be given our head, our independence, our freedom from God, if we were to grow up and finally discover our true freedom in God. The Prodigal Son had to go away in order to return, in order to receive the fullness of his father's love: a fullness which his elder brother, safely at home, could not experience. The Easter Liturgy makes the same point:

> O happy fault, o necessary sin of Adam,
> which gained for us so great a Redeemer!

God has not made a perfect world which he is now carelessly allowing us to spoil; rather he is still at work with his smelly and messy materials, fashioning mankind and all creation into the sort of thing he has in mind. The creation is incomplete; we are still somewhere on the sixth day of it, the divine Friday, with the longed-for rest and re-creation still eluding us, ahead around the corner. Genesis 1:1—2:3 gives us the blueprint, an overview of the whole process; but from Genesis 2:4 up to the present day (with the doubtful exception of Revelation and some of the more prophetic bits in the Prophets) we are then plunged sharply back into the middle of the story, from a bird's-eye to a worm's-eye view; into the tears, sweat and blood of everyday reality.

We haven't yet arrived in the Kingdom of our true humanity: but Jesus – the 'second Adam', the 'Proper Man', the 'first-fruits' – announces, by his life and by his preaching, its coming realization; and his Eucharist anticipates and celebrates that reality. Where Christ has gone before in glory, we follow in hope. And the 'daily bread' – more accurately, the 'bread of tomorrow' – which we receive, empowers us to anticipate Christ's Kingdom in our lives also, to revive the insipid present with the salt and leaven of eternity. If we truly enter into the Eucharist, we in our turn can *become* daily bread for the world.

But this invitation and challenge to share in the adventure of God's life has often been too strong for the Church. We have preferred to remain outside, at a safe distance, seeing the

Holy Trinity as a closed shop, a beautiful but inaccessible system away beyond the heaven of heavens. This has been especially true in our Western thinking, influenced as it is by that small but devastating phrase 'filioque' which surreptitiously slithered into our Creed at some point in the first millennium. The original version has the Holy Spirit 'proceeding from the Father' only: in the West he (or she) 'proceeds from the Father *and the Son*'. There sits the Father, on his heavenly throne; at his right, the ascended Christ; and, proceeding from the pair of them, the Holy Spirit – as one especially unfortunate hymn puts it,

O heav'nly Dove,
Praise to thee, fruit of their love . . .

The trouble with this picture is the divide it creates between Jesus and the rest of us: it is an *inhospitable* picture. He's up there, we're down here; he's divine, we're human; he dispenses the Spirit, we receive it. He is the Champion, the undisputed Son of God: we are miserable sinners, who might just make it to heaven by some complicated system of salvation – but, even then, only on suffrance, only as 'adopted children'. And then again, maybe we won't make it . . . what does it depend on? Being good and keeping the rules? (but we'll never manage that). Being predestined to grace? (but suppose we aren't? and how do we know?) Being 'born again' by a conversion experience? (but what if one of those doesn't come our way, or we just aren't that kind of person?) It's a recipe for despair.

What is more, suppose we do make it to heaven, suppose we do get to resemble this other-worldly Jesus . . . the trouble is, the more we become like him, the less we shall be like anyone else. Being Christian will mean being *more than* human, *other than* ordinarily human. We end up with different breeds, the saved and the unsaved. And it is not a very big step from there (and it is a step many have taken) to discounting the non-Christians as *less than* human: to embracing a cosy Christian fascism, the ultimate inhospitality.

The idea of Christians as a different breed is rather rife in our Western Church today. People who attend church either feel smug because they *are* different, or guilty because they *aren't* different, from everyone else (quite often offloading that guilt on to the minister: well, at least *he* can be different, and woe betide him if he isn't!) Non-churchgoers also often feel there should be a difference, a feeling they express either in a vague guilt about not going to church, or in anger that those who do go are as bad as everyone else: hypocrites!

This divorcing of heaven from earth, of Jesus from the rest of us, is often reflected in our worship, including the Eucharist: everything goes on *up there*; all the glory is focused on the sanctuary, the priest, the pulpit, the preacher; the congregation is passive, bored. And recent liturgical reform has sadly often left the priest more cut off and exalted than before; on a huge podium, without even servers or subdeacons to represent the laity, alone beyond the immutable altar. No divine hospitality here, no sharing of the Spirit.

There are two major moments in the New Testament story when the Holy Spirit is given: at the baptism of Jesus,[10] and after his resurrection.[11] Taken separately, these stories might indeed suggest that Jesus is on a different plane from the rest of us: at his baptism he alone is acclaimed as the Beloved Son; later, he alone issues the Spirit, while everyone else receives it.[12]

But the two events should not be taken separately – as St Luke makes very clear. His 'Gospel' is in two volumes: the first (Luke) tells the story of the earthly Jesus; the second (Acts) that of the Church, the extended Body of Christ. There are significant parallels between the two books: both involve miracles, martyrdom and journeys; both begin with an angelic promise. And, at about the same stage in each volume, the Holy Spirit is given: at the descent of the dove on Jesus in Luke chapter 3, and through the wind and fire of Pentecost in Acts chapter 2. These two stories also should be taken in parallel. Jesus' mission stems from his baptism, the Church's mission from Pentecost; in volume 1 it is Jesus who receives the Spirit, in volume 2 it is the whole Church. At Pentecost, he is not dispensing the Spirit from an exalted position of exclusive sonship, but making us a party to his own baptism:

the Spirit and the sonship are one. His ascension has not cut him off from the rest of us, only enabled him more completely to share his gifts; as Ephesians puts it,

> To each one of us grace has been given,
> according to the measure of the gift of Christ . . .
> 'Going up into the heights he took captivity captive,
> he gave gifts to men and women.' (4:7–8)

Pentecost makes clear the true meaning of Jesus' baptism. Jesus has been revealed as the Son of God, the receiver of the Holy Spirit; but the revelation, far from shutting the rest of us out ('this, as opposed to the rest of you, is my beloved Son') is rather a sign of hope: 'This is my beloved child, and so shall you all be.' For the very act of baptism was a sign of Jesus' utter giving away of himself, his refusal of all privilege, his irrevocable solidarity with mankind.

It is Matthew who brings this out most fully in his account (3:13–17). When Jesus comes to be baptized, John recoils in horror: You, Lord, baptized by me? You, the Son of God, making yourself subordinate to me? It should be the other way around! . . . like Peter at the Last Supper: You, Lord, washing my feet? Never![13] But, here as there, Jesus insists: Yes, let it be so; I want no privileges, my vocation is to total humanity. And this is ratified in the story of his temptations in the wilderness,[14] where he resists every suggestion of becoming Superman, choosing instead the way of full humanity, which inevitably becomes the Way of the Cross.

St Paul, in a famous passage to the Philippians, expresses in a hymn just what Matthew is saying in this story:

> [Jesus], being in the form of God,
> did not think that to be equal with God meant a snatching,
> but emptied himself, taking the form of a slave,
> being in the likeness of men and women,
> and, being found in shape as a human being,
> became obedient as far as death, the death of the cross.
> (2:6–8)

Being divine didn't mean snatching for privilege: on the contrary, it meant self-abasement, total identification with others, pouring oneself out in love. And this is precisely what he was doing at his baptism; and it is *precisely* at this moment, the moment of his refusal of all privilege, that the Spirit descends and the voice is heard. It is when he embraces the life of solidarity and self-sacrifice that Jesus is acclaimed as the beloved Son of God; for, contrary to popular belief, that is what a Son of God looks like.

The moment of revelation did not show Jesus encased in some heavenly bubble: aha, he is not an ordinary human being after all! It is not the revelation of an alien – put on the right spectacles and you'll see him in all his alienness; if things get tough he can always spirit himself safely away from the human arena. No: it is exactly when he says 'I am in it with you', when he refuses privilege, when he humbles himself with no turning back, that he is acclaimed as God's Son. He wasn't an idealized King David, or a Greek god, or Rambo or Superman. Indeed, he displayed as many 'feminine' qualities as 'masculine' ones, and the overriding message which he preached, lived and died was: If you want to live, die; if you want to receive, give; if you want to find yourself, lose yourself.

Jesus is no alien divinity in disguise for a rescue mission; he is Son of God not *in spite of* his humanity, but *by virtue of* his full and total and unabated humanity. If he had been less human – if he had after all agreed to baptize John, done the odd miracle in the wildnerness, encouraged people to advertise his messiahship, let Peter wash his feet, come down from the cross – then he would have been less, not more, divine. The voice from heaven vindicated his initial act of solidarity and self-giving; the resurrection vindicated his final one.

Jesus is the Icon of our humanity: like an icon, he shows us the full meaning of what is there; but, like an icon also, he invites us to participate in the mystery, to enter in and place ourselves where he is. He is Lord; but, in Anglo-Saxon at least, 'Lord' means 'the one who shares bread with his people'. The Messiah *whose very messiahship consisted in giving himself away* could not possibly have been jealous of his status; for the whole purpose of his life was to share it, to invite us on equal terms into his Kingdom.

The Gospel, therefore, is an account of this divine and sacrificial hospitality. God is inviting us to the banquet of his Kingdom; Jesus embodies the invitation, in his teaching and in the living out of his life. Continually he breaks down the traditional barriers, scandalously including in his circle those who had seemed irredeemable, beyond the pale; demonstrating a divine love that knows no pale. And, when he accepts hospitality from unlikely people, it is really he who is giving God's hospitality to them: to the woman at the well,[15] to Zacchaeus,[16] to the woman who anoints him,[17] to the disciples at Emmaus.[18] 'This man receives sinners and eats with them.'[19] Reverse perspective is at work again; the true host is Jesus, inviting us into the picture.

But his hospitality is never given without cost. In so many stories we can feel what it cost him, always allowing people in, never saying 'enough's enough'. We may well sympathize with Tim Rice's *Jesus Christ Superstar* when, overwhelmed with the demands being made on him, he rounds on the crowds and sends them packing; but it is at just this point in the musical that we realize for certain we aren't dealing with the Jesus of the Gospels. He never turned people away, whatever it cost: he just went on pouring out his life. To turn people away would have been to make stones into bread, to come down from the cross.

And the sadness of more than one parable, like the story of the Great Supper – such a wonderful feast, and people just won't come to it, like Edward Lear's ice cream, which

Nobody tasted,
and so it was wasted –

must reflect Jesus' own sadness at the failure of his message of welcoming love. 'He came to his own, but his own received him not'; he poured his whole life out for them as a sign of the richness God was offering, but they weren't interested, indeed they treated the message with contempt, just as in the parable they

made light of it and went off,
one to his farm, another to his business,

11

while the rest seized his servants,
treated them shamefully, and killed them.[20]

Three stories speak most clearly of Jesus' divine hospitality,
and as clearly of its cost. Mark's account of the Feeding of
the Five Thousand (6:31–44) comes straight after a most
hectic and worrying time: John the Baptist has just been
beheaded, Jesus and the disciples have been so busy that they
'had no leisure even to eat'. The reader positively sighs with
relief when at last they get away in their boat for a well-
earned rest in a lonely place, and it seems unbearable that,
when they get there, they find they aren't alone but thronged
by crowds from all the towns round about. Yet Jesus accepts
the situation; 'he had compassion on them, because they were
like sheep without a shepherd'; he feeds their spiritual needs
with his teaching, and *even then* he won't send them away:
without having eaten anything himself, he demonstrates in
the miracle the superabundant hospitality of God.

The second story is that of the marriage at Cana in John
2. Here again, Jesus answers a human need with extravagant
divine bounty, and – though more subtly this time – again
the miracle depends on his own suffering. When Mary tells
him about the lack of wine, Jesus rounds on her: 'Woman,
what have I got to do with you?' Why *is* he so rude? Numerous
commentators and translators have explained away, or toned
down, the force of his words; they still sound rude to me. And
surely it is because she has reminded him of his 'hour', of his
coming sacrifice; he can give them what they want, yes, but
not by waving a magic wand, only by pouring himself out.
So, later in the same Gospel, Jesus reveals himself as the
source of living water, as the Bread on which God's people
must feed; later still, blood and water come cascading from
his side. The good wine at the wedding prefigures this, it costs
him everything; and (John tells us) the miracle 'manifests his
glory', a motif which takes us back to the glory of the Word in
chapter 1, but which later comes to describe the approaching
sacrifice on the cross.

Both these stories have a clear eucharistic reference, Jesus
giving himself as bread and as wine. In the third major

account of his hospitality the reference is clearer still, for it is the story of the Last Supper.[21] Here again, he seems to be receiving hospitality but is actually giving it. Again he gives bread and wine to his friends; again, what he is really giving is himself, the gift he is pouring out takes its meaning from the forthcoming sacrifice. But whereas in the other two stories the cost to himself was veiled, here it is made explicit: this *is* my Body which I am giving, he says; this *is* my Blood which I am pouring out. The next day he is dead.

And in the Eucharist, as Paul says, we 'show forth his death',[22] we sum up his self-giving: the pouring out of his life in his teaching and in his signs; at the Last Supper, on the cross, at Pentecost. But we also respond to his hospitality and receive what has been poured out, the 'power to become children of God'.[23] Since Pentecost, that final act of hospitality in the New Testament drama, the splendour once focused on Jesus alone has been available to all. He has poured himself out, not as a divine demonstration, certainly not to propitiate divine anger: but so that we too may become the sons and daughters of God, growing up into the fullness of our creation, the 'measure of the stature of the fullness of Christ'.[24]

So the Eucharist makes no sense unless we are drawn into it. It is not to be contemplated from outside, a ritual enacted by the priest, something which God inexorably demands or magically gives, which may or may not be 'valid'. Our offering of word, bread and wine cannot be separated from the offering of ourselves and our humanity: the gifts of word, bread and wine which we receive will only be effective if we are open, however inadequately, to God's Spirit.

The Eucharist makes no sense, either, apart from our ordinary lives. What we offer is not just our temporary, religious, Sunday-morning selves, but our whole selves, our whole life, with all its tedium and ructions and silliness and incomprehension; what we receive back is not a Sunday suit for the soul, a Christian lifejacket against the buffetings of the world, but the gift of Christ, life in all its fullness and abundance and glory; something unlikely to be neat or easily understood.

13

For Christ's invitation is to take the plunge, not into religion but into life, and the greatest division within humanity is not between those who go to church and those who don't, Christians and non-Christians, the religious and the secular: but between those who continue on the surface of life and those who have dared to go beneath the surface and face what they find there, whatever name they may give it. Baptism is the outward sign of this plunge, this breaking out of the captivity of convention, through the Red Sea and into the wilderness where nothing is easy any more, but God is real and the Promised Land does lie somewhere ahead; and the Eucharist is our manna for the journey, the spiritual food which keeps us on the move, preventing our slide back to easier gods, whetting our appetite for the milk and honey ahead.

'Manna' is Hebrew for 'what is it?'[25] And the Eucharist, too, like the whole Christian enterprise, is more of a question than an answer. It may sometimes make us feel fulfilled and deeply glad; but never merely comfortable. So, in this book, the idea is not to give any definitive description of it, only to open up some questions it asks. For the only possible *answer* to these questions is in the living of our lives, accompanied by the life of Christ.

The Eucharist is not a bald affirmation: this is how it is, take it or leave it. It is also an anticipation, an expression of hope: this is how it shall be, alleluia. It is a cry: O Lord, have mercy; O Lord, how long? It is a pledge, the rededication of God's people to his will and his Kingdom. And it is an empowering: not just our Yes to God, but also his Yes to us, as he frees us from sin, strengthens us with his word and communion, and renews us for our final communion with Christ in the life of the Trinity, the Kingdom of Heaven.

All of which may sound wonderful; but also, perhaps – in a world of sin, brokenness, fallibility, pomposity and extreme silliness (qualities which infect the whole of life, including the Church *and* the Eucharist) – unrealistic and absurd. But then, absurdity, foolishness, fragility: these are bound to be a part of our Christian character, as long as we are called to be prophets of glory in a messy world, as long as we are called

14

to celebrate the Sabbath while it is still actually Friday. Living and speaking as the first-fruits of redeemed humanity in an unredeemed world led Jesus inevitably to the cross: the route is no different for us. Whatever we do or say will be absurd and precarious, but, in the very end, perhaps also worthwhile, as Paul says again and again to the Corinthians:

We have this treasure in vessels of earthenware,
so that the overflowing of power may be of God and not from us:
in everything hard-pressed but not hemmed in,
perplexed but not despairing,
persecuted but not abandoned,
struck down but not destroyed,
always carrying the deadness of Jesus around in our body,
so that the life of Jesus, too, may be manifested in our body.[26]

1   C. S. Lewis; *The Voyage of the Dawn Treader* (Puffin Books 1952), pp. 11–16.
2   John 1:1.
3   John 1:12.
4   John 1:38–39.
5   1 Corinthians 12:12–27; Romans 12:4–5.
6   John 15:1–6.
7   1 Peter 2:4–5.
8   Genesis 18:1–15.
9   This is one of the suggested greetings for the beginning of the Roman Catholic Mass. The commoner alternative 'The Lord be with you – and also with you' seems thinner, but still conveys the welcome.
10 Mark 1:9–11; Matthew 3:13–17; Luke 3:21–22; and, by implication, John 1:29–34.
11 Acts 2:1–4; John 20:19–23. John puts the giving of the Spirit to the Apostles in a quite different setting from the better known story of Pentecost in Acts, but makes it equally plain that it represents a sharing of Jesus' vocation: 'Just as the Father has sent me, I too am sending you.'
12 See Acts 2:33.

13 John 13:6–8.
14 Matthew 4:1–11, Luke 4:1–13.
15 John 4:7–15.
16 Luke 19:1–10.
17 Luke 7:36–50, cf. Mark 14:3–9, John 12:1–8.
18 Luke 24:28–31.
19 Luke 15:2.
20 Matthew 22:5–6, cf. Luke 14:18–20.
21 Mark 14:12–25 and parallels.
22 1 Corinthians 11:26.
23 John 1:12.
24 Ephesians 4:13, cf. 15–16.
25 See Exodus 16:15.
26 2 Corinthians 4:7–10.

2

Kyrie
The Cry for Healing

The Eucharist begins with a welcome: but the mood soon changes. As Jesus went from his baptism into a time of fasting, then began his ministry by preaching repentance;[1] so the first main section of the Eucharist is the 'penitential rite', summed up by Greek words that echo down the centuries: *Kyrie eleison, Christe eleison, Kyrie eleison!* – Lord have mercy, Christ have mercy, Lord have mercy!

We are called to be God's children: but we mustn't be smug about it, for our creation is not yet complete. To use another image, we are still, like the Israelites in Exodus, on our way through the wilderness; it was not so much Jordan that we crossed at our baptism, as the Red Sea. As we contemplate the enormous distance that still lies ahead of us, the enormous gap between our true humanity, revealed in Christ, and the grubby thing which passes for humanity now, there is no possible cause for self-satisfaction – indeed, we might well fall prey to the opposite and equally appalling temptation, despair.

But, for Christians, the antidote to smugness isn't despair. We don't have to go on lurching between these two horrors, like Alice who kept on growing too tall or too short, too tall to get through the gate, too short to reach the key of the garden.[3] The antidote to smugness is *penitence*: penitence alone will open the narrow gate into the garden of new life. For penitence takes account both of our human malaise, our sinfulness, our failure to live in the image of God; and also of our dissatisfaction, our longing for something better, our

17

heartfelt desire to become whole and to enter the Kingdom. Penitence is the song of the pilgrim, far from home, but still on the way. It can never be smug, because it takes sin seriously; but it can never be gloomy, because it issues in forgiveness.

So, as the full immensity of what it means to come into God's presence dawns upon us, penitence is the first mood to be evoked; as, indeed, a turning from sin to Christ has always been integral to the rite of Baptism. The Eucharist begins, as it were, with a renewal of baptismal vows; and the Roman missal still allows for the sprinkling with holy water, a more direct reminder of Baptism, as an alternative to the spoken penitential rite. But, whether the words are spoken, sung or silent, we begin with a poignant cry for mercy, forgiveness and new life: *Kyrie eleison!*

And probably our penitence should be directed first towards the Church itself, so far away is it from fulfilling its true vocation to be the Body of Christ in the world. Christ is the first-fruits; yes, and with all our modern insistence on Jesus as a man of his times, with all our doubts about his miraculousness, still it does not seem absurd to speak of this man as the Son of God, as the Proper Man. But as for us, as for the Church! We no more seem to resemble the first or even the second fruits of the Kingdom than we have sprouted wings and harps and haloes.

Our apostasy, unfaithfulness, has been terrible. We are indeed 'hypocrites' (the Greek word means 'actors'), affirming one thing but displaying another; pretending to be the bearers of salvation, the Body of Christ who suffered for the world, yet behaving not just 'no better than anyone else' (which would at least be refreshingly incarnational), but so often actually *worse* than the rest, fiddling with our petty rituals and preoccupations and infightings while Rome burns, while the world suffers . . .

There is a searing moment (perhaps a touch too searing) in Thomas Hardy's *Jude the Obscure*, where Jude finds that his children have committed mass suicide, and, still reeling from the horror of it, he hears two clergymen pass beneath his window, discussing 'the Eastward position', a nice point of liturgical controversy. 'Good God!' cries Jude, 'The Eastward position! and all creation groaning!'[4] ... a bit overdone, maybe, but still uncomfortably near the bone: only nowadays it would be *The Mass in Latin!* or *The Alternative Service Book!* or *The validity of women priests!* or *Infant baptism!* or *The inerrancy of Scripture!* or *Speaking in tongues!* ... and all creation groaning! There isn't a Christian group in the world which doesn't have its equivalent of The Eastward Position to get worked up about as a way of escaping the groans of creation. But our true calling is to hear those groans and respond to them; so we must identify our apostasy, and cry *Kyrie eleison!*

The Church's apostasy takes different forms in its different branches; we all trivialize the Gospel in one way or another, and it isn't for me to point the finger at any particular instance. What must be pointed out, however, is a fairly general trivialization of penitence itself.

The power to forgive sins is one of Christ's great gifts to his Church. It is wonderfully liberating, when weighed down by a sense of sin, to be able to bring it all to the surface and be assured of forgiveness, like lancing a boil, like the purgative of which David sings:

Purge me with hyssop, and I shall be clean:
    wash me, and I shall be whiter than snow.
Fill me with joy and gladness:
    let the bones which you have broken rejoice ...
Create in me a clean heart, O God:
    and put a new and right spirit within me.[5]

The Sacrament of personal Confession, though it has often been abused and misunderstood, has enormous potential for healing; and the General Confession at the start of the Eucharist can give a similar, though less profound, sense of individual forgiveness.

But the act of penitence can easily become a formality. There is so little time to reflect on our sins: and, if we are honest, we may often feel that these aren't so terribly grievous. General Confession and Absolution doesn't appear to go all that deep: and it has dangers. Jesus told a story of two men in the Temple, praying: the Pharisee, up front, saying Thank you, God, there are no flies on *me*! thank you, God, I've got nothing to confess, not like this publican . . . and the publican, crouching at the back, muttering almost inaudibly Lord, have mercy on me, a sinner; Lord, have mercy on me, a sinner!⁶ Now, of course, the very suggestion of penitence helps guard us against the smugness of the Pharisee, so certain that he is justified before God; but isn't there a subtler danger, that we become a sort of hybrid? praying Lord, have mercy on me, a sinner, so that, when you have had mercy, I may become like this Pharisee. Whereas our vocation is always to stay, with Christ, among the sinners.

The danger is of a too easy forgiveness, a too light healing of the wound. For one thing, who am I to assess my own sins, to know which are the grave ones and which the petty?

> Once in a contrite passion
> I cried out in my grief,
> And said 'O Lord, have mercy!
> Of sinners I am chief!'
> Then came a kindly angel,
> And, standing just behind,
> Said, 'Vanity, my little man:
> You're nothing of the kind!'⁷

For me to judge my own sins would be like a physician healing himself, or a poet explaining her own poetry: others usually see so much better, from a distance. The things that worry me most may actually be rather unimportant; while my gravest sins may in fact be things that hardly occur to me, even things I'm not aware of.

The Church has much to answer for here. Traditionally we come down so hard on the individual misdemeanours, especially of course anything to do with sex: so that, in popular speech, 'sin' has actually come to mean sexual naughtiness; and whole lives have been ruined by the hangups and guilt complexes so created. How mercilessly we condemn, say, a priest who has momentarily succumbed to sexual temptation; and how blithely, at the same time, we turn a blind eye to those who pollute the world or invest their money in the misery of others, through arms sales or exploited labour. When Christian leaders pronounce on the evils of society, so often they don't mean racialism, unemployment, warmongering, or exploitation: they mean drug abuse or black magic or pornography. Not that these things aren't sinful; but they are only the symptoms of a far deeper sickness.

It's so much more comfortable to stay on the surface, condemning others for their vicious practices, but ourselves remaining on the right side of God (barring the odd little lapse, which Confession can soon put right) thanking him, indeed, that we aren't like these others . . . and back we walk again, before we've even noticed, up the garden path and through the Pharisee's front door.

Whereas, if we look below the surface at the real evils of society, we have to admit what we all know deep down: that we are *all* part of this sin, we *all* need grace, my neighbour's sin is my sin too, I too am partly responsible for the evils of the world; and that, when I see a rapist or a prostitute, a drug addict or a child batterer – even, forsooth, a racialist or an arms dealer – there indeed, but for the grace of God, go I.[8]

For, when the Church assembles and cries *Kyrie eleison!*, we are so much more than a collection of individuals, each recalling her or his individual sins, and each receiving her or his individual, pre-packaged absolution. We come together, not as a bunch of individually wrapped sinners, but as the Body of Christ and the priest of the world, confessing to God a sin of which our poor little misdemeanours may be temporary and superficial expressions, but which actually goes far, far deeper, and which won't be much affected by merely removing the symptoms. It is as if my sins and your sins were separate patches of damp appearing on a church wall, and we were satisfying ourselves by repainting the individual patches rather than attacking the trouble at its source. The innocent-looking blade of couch-grass on the surface, if I dig at it rather than cutting it off, leads to a whole alarming labyrinth of roots below.

'My' sins are not really mine: most of them I share with

most people, and all of them are a manifestation of the 'orig-inal sin', the general malaise, which we all inherit and have to put up with until the day of Christ. So, as a Christian, as a member of Christ's Body, my true reason for confessing my personal sins is less to make me feel better than to lead me down to an acknowledgement and understanding and compassion for the sins of all mankind. And *this* is what we should be offering to God as our Eucharist begins. When we say, sing, cry *Kyrie eleison!*, we are repeating, or rather joining in, what Christ does as the Lamb of God[9] and the world's High Priest:[10] we are offering to God, in solidarity and in penitence, the sin of all the world; not in gloom and despair, but in the confidence of his forgiveness, mercy and healing – of the coming new Creation.

Once we have moved beyond a merely individual penitence towards this priestly offering of all the world's sin, it turns out to be both Bad News and Good News. The *bad news* is that instant forgiveness is out; there is no longer any possibility of just saying the right words, or conjuring up the right mood, and so finding ourselves up front with the Pharisee. To know we can be made clean, to experience the reality of God's forgiving love: these things, when they come home to us, as they occasionally do, are of course wonderful and life-giving; but, even so, they are more a refreshing sign of future sal-vation – like the signs of Jesus himself – than any cause for complacency now. As soon as we take on board not just our own sinfulness but *the sin of the world*, we lose all possibility of instant salvation.

For, even if by any chance we were to stray across Jordan into the Promised Land, we would have no business to remain there; any more than Jesus himself made a song and dance about his special standing with God. When he plunges into the Jordan, it is not to escape from the wilderness: on the contrary, he is setting aside his security to be with his people in their wilderness of temptation and wandering and lostness. Refusing all privilege, he so identifies himself with the dark-ness and sin of the world that, in Paul's daring phrase, he is 'made *to be sin*',[11] that, according to the Apostles' Creed, he

'descends into hell'. And this is the direction of all his ministry: continually identifying, and identified, with the sinners;
continually seeking what is lost; continually challenging those
still on the safe side to plunge in, lose their life and follow
him.

As we respond to that challenge and follow the logic of our
own baptism, we find ourselves being led in the same direction. We can't boast of our own forgiveness and salvation
while others grope about in the darkness (even assuming that
we are really more in the light than they); we can only plunge
back into the darkness to share our salvation with them, as
Christ has shared his sonship with us. In any case, our salvation depends on theirs: *we can't be saved on our own*, it's a
contradiction in terms. There simply cannot be a time, in this
life or beyond it (*pace* C. S. Lewis[12] and the Book of Revelation[13]) when we, and God, finally shrug our shoulders and
say 'Well, too bad, they've had every chance; from now on
they must make do with darkness, flames, and the gnashing
of teeth, or else our heavenly banquet may get cold'. The
heavenly banquet can be no banquet with half the guests
missing.

Once our confession of sin becomes an identification with
the sin of the world, we shall find ourselves impossibly grimy,
and it will take more than the words of Absolution to get us
clean again: it will take a long and dangerous journey through
the desert to the very waters of life. Our cleansing has become
inseparable from other people's; we cannot, and we do not
wish to, leave the back of the Temple, until all our fellow-
publicans in the world can come with us.

The sin we confess is corporate, and that is bad news for our
hopes of instant personal redemption. But the *good news* is
that now, at last, we can escape from the crushing idea that
sin is all our fault; that confessing sins means weighing ourselves down with guilt. The doctrine of 'original sin', properly
understood, is not a cause for doom and gloom: it is a positive
liberation! If I had been born in the Garden of Eden, then
any sinfulness on my part would be inexcusable and damn-
able: but as (according to this doctrine) I have actually been

23

born into an imperfect, 'fallen', world, where everything (including me) is pretty fundamentally out of joint; then surely I can hardly bear all the blame and the guilt for what goes wrong in my world or my life, even for those sins I seem deliberately to commit?

We repeatedly hear of court cases where a person pleads not innocence but diminished responsibility, on the grounds of a poor upbringing, or brain damage, or an extra Y chromosome. And, if it was a matter of upbringing, of lack of love, say, in early childhood, the fashion is then to blame the parents: 'Obviously he stood no chance with parents like that.' But what about the parents? What was *their* upbringing like? Why should they be dubbed any more wilfully evil than their offspring? So where did it all really start? Who is *ultimately* to blame?

Sin, in traditional Christian terms, is separation: from God, from one another, from our truest selves. This is something we manifestly can't help: the very acts of being born and weaned involve a separation, a tearing apart; and the cosmic birth we call creation, and the cosmic weaning we call freedom – what a tearing apart these have entailed! The story is told of creation one day, sin the next day; but then it is in the nature of stories to separate out things that finally belong together – the cross and the resurrection, the ascension and Pentecost. Mightn't it be that creation and the Fall actually go together too, that you couldn't have one without the other?

In which case, if anyone is ultimately responsible for sin, blasphemous though it may sound, it must be God: if he has made the world, he is accountable for the world as it is, sin and all. The ultimate blame cannot be mankind's, and it certainly cannot be mine. I am the agent, the means, the victim of sin: but I am not its originator.

This may sound very like the diseased slogan of many modern politicians: *Never admit that anything is your fault!* In fact, it is the very opposite, for, whereas the 'politician' excuses herself by blaming others ('blaming is a way of making yourself feel better by making other people feel worse'[14]), we begin by saying No one is to blame. That is an infinitely compassionate beginning. I once heard a devotional address given at short notice by a venerable Cowley Father. 'Sin . . . sin . . .', he kept saying; 'well, there it is.' And that is where we begin: sin is just there, it's a fact of life, it's not anyone's fault in particular, and there's no point in getting ourselves or anyone else all guilty or worked up about it.

That's where we begin; but that is *not* where we stop. Another fashionable political view is that, because sin and selfishness are so much a fact of life, so entirely *ingrained* in human nature, the only realistic way forward is to 'work with the grain', to give free rein to our 'natural' instincts: greed, self-seeking and the desire for power. Such (we are told) is true freedom, and any attempt to build on a higher view of human nature is 'utopian'. Some politicians express this view in overtly theological terms: if the Church criticizes the rule of the mighty, if the Church indeed expresses any political point of view whatsoever (other than approval of the *status quo*), then the Church is being utopian, forgetting the doctrine of original sin, and neglecting its real calling to bring individuals back to God.

But, while our Gospel does indeed begin by acknowledging sin, by taking it entirely seriously as a given thing of our existence, the next most certain of all things after death itself – 'there it is' – under no circumstances does it stop there. Yes, sin is *ingrained* in human nature, but it is not *the grain of* human nature. In Narnian terminology, sin is the 'deep magic from the dawn of time': but our hope is in the 'deeper magic from before the dawn of time',[15] from beyond the gates of time. We perceive our true, original and final humanity not in the sinful, fallen nature of Adam, but in the glorious, divine humanity of Christ. Because Christ is the 'Proper Man', our brother; because 'we are to be like him';[16] we dare to assert a hope for humanity beyond the reign of sin.

Utopianism pretends there is no sin: get society right, and people will become like angels, all our problems will be over. Christianity acknowledges sin – 'there it is' – but then proclaims its faith in the Lamb of God who takes sin away. And, because we are his Body, his heirs, his co-workers, it is now time for us to play our part, to take the world's sin upon ourselves in order that it may be taken away. So we begin our Eucharist, our celebration of Christ, by crying, for ourselves and for our world, *Kyrie eleison!*

Sin was not Jesus' fault, yet he immersed himself in it totally and offered it to God 'with loud cries and tears';[17] it isn't particularly much our fault either, but so what? Our calling is to accept not the blame, but the *responsibility* for our sin and the world's sin, looking not backwards but ahead: and so to break the vicious circle of its dominion. Sin perpetuates itself – as we see all too clearly, for example, in Northern Ireland – by feeding on our desire to be in the right, so that from one person, group, generation to another we pass on the blame, the guilt, the sickness, the unforgiving hatred . . . and the only way through is the narrow, crazy, impossible, crucifying, yet utterly simple way of Christ: to turn the whole vortex upside down and inside out, seeking not blame but healing, not sacrifice but mercy, not the punishment of our enemies but their forgiveness.

This is powerfully expressed in Alan Garner's extraordinary story, *The Owl Service*. Three teenagers, spending a summer together in the claustrophobic atmosphere of a Welsh valley, find a dinner service in the attic, and discover a way of tracing out its floral pattern that turns the flowers into owls. This somehow unleashes upon them a pattern of jealousy and, finally, hatred – represented by the claws and beaks of the owls – which has repeated itself in the same valley over and over again for generations. In the closing scene the girl, Alison, is being so torn apart by this jealousy that claw marks actually start to appear on her body, and the air is filled with feathers. Then, all at once, one of the boys, Roger, sees what is the matter. He goes up to Alison and pronounces a word of penitence and forgiveness:

'She's not owls, she's flowers . . .
. . . Flowers, flowers. That's the way.' The marks paled on her skin, and the tightness went from her face as she breathed to the measure of his hand on her brow. 'That's better. There now: yes: yes: of course they're flowers . . . Why didn't you cut the pattern into flowers right at the

26

start, you silly girl?' . . . And the room was full of petals
from skylight and rafters, and all about them a fragrance,
and petals, flowers falling, broom, meadowsweet, falling,
flowers of the oak.[18]

Not owls, but flowers: forgiveness is the key. Yet the forgiveness for which we thirst so often seems beyond us, something
we just can't manage. 'Forgive us our sins as we forgive those
who sin against us': can this really mean God won't forgive
us till we have forgiven others? But how can we forgive at all
unless we first know his forgiveness? Doesn't it rather mean
'Let your forgiveness flow through me and from me to others;
let me be the instrument, the channel of your forgiveness and
peace'? The servant in Matthew 18:23–35 was uncondition-
ally forgiven; his downfall came because he wouldn't pass
his master's forgiveness on to his fellow servant. By turning
towards others in forgiveness, we are in fact and at the same
time turning towards God in contrition.

Forgiveness is a stream: this comes out also in the story of
the sinful woman who anoints Jesus at the house of Simon
the Pharisee, in Luke 7:36–50. It is one of those stories that
doesn't quite seem to fit together. The woman wets Jesus'
feet with her tears, and wipes them with her hair, and kisses
his feet and anoints him with ointment; and Simon mutters
to himself that if Jesus were a real prophet he would have
known she was a sinner and kept her away. And Jesus
responds with the story of the two debtors, the one who is
forgiven more ending up with a greater love for his master.

The trouble is this: Jesus' *action*, following the woman's
heartfelt display of love, suggests that *she has been forgiven
because of her love*: whereas the *parable* suggests the very
opposite, that *her love is the result of her forgiveness*. Critics have
been quick to mark this down as a 'crux', an ill-thought-out
conflation of two separate stories: but mightn't that be a little
too logical? The love of the woman, and the forgiveness she
receives, are not two separate things at all, one caused by the
other: they are two aspects of a single event (which, once
again, a story has separated out). The act of love *is* an act of
repentance; the giving and the receiving are one. The trouble

27

with poor Simon is that he has neither given nor received. The woman has repented by turning to Christ in love; so we are forgiven as we turn to others in forgiveness.

Kyrie eleison! What richness lies within this prayer, the prayer of the penitent Church across the world and down the ages, voiced in those two same and so resonant Greek words, with their overtones of the oil of mercy and gladness. Lord, have mercy: you forgive us, your forgiveness spreads infinitely; we will radiate that forgiveness upon others, as we also ask their forgiveness; and we will forgive ourselves also, even dare to admit our anger and forgive you . . .

The confession of sin is an acceptance of responsibility; but, beyond that, it can awaken in us a deep desire for things to be set right. Just as pain, in a healthy person, is a useful warning that something is wrong: so, rightly channelled, my sense of personal sin can lead me on to a sense of responsibility and compassion for the corporate sin besetting my world. I feel out of joint; and I recognize in that feeling the out-of-jointness of the world at every level. Nothing (beginning with me) is really quite as it could be, if only . . .

Our penitence has begun with ourselves and our Church: 'Lord, convert the world and begin with me, with us.' But it must lead on to the groans of creation, to a deep expression of compassion for the world for which we now bear responsibility, God's glorious world, ravaged by sin. Our *Kyrie* must take in not only the personal and shared sin of those in Church, but also the sin of the world whose priest we are, the sin of mankind, more terrible and rampant now than ever. We must confess the pollution and devastation that stem from our greed; the wars, and the rumour of still more terrible wars, stemming from our pride; the appalling injustice between the rich and the poor, the powerful and the powerless; and the crippling despair that infects both rich and poor:

Look around you, can you see?
Times are troubled, people grieve.

28

See the violence, feel the hardness;
all my people, weep with me.
Kyrie eleison, Christe eleison, Kyrie eleison.[19]

As we contemplate this mystery of sin, suffering, evil in our world; as we consider how wrong things have gone, how out of joint they are, within us, among us and all around us; the hopes gone grey, the loveliness that has passed, the joy that has escaped; what a great sadness is awakened. And if we were Stoic philosophers, no doubt we would stay with the sadness, content at last to live with it and to take what comes. But we aren't Stoics, we are Christians: and we face the sin of the world, not with despair, not with wry resignation, but with faith, beneath and beyond it all, in a living, creating and redeeming God; a faith which may itself help us face reality better than many.

For our faith tells us we *are* bound for the Promised Land; that mankind *is* to be redeemed into God's image; that the creation *is* to reflect, and resound to, his glory. Our sadness is not hopeless regret for the unattainable, but a deep *longing* for the Kingdom, for the state of affairs where God reigns, where sin is not the final reality, where people *are* conformed to the image of Christ. When ever will the gap be bridged, the valley filled in, between things as they are and things as they might be, if only . . .?

This tension between what is, and what could or should be, can awaken in us a terrible and destructive guilt: but once we accept the givenness of sin, and so replace guilt with longing, blame with responsibility; once we begin to live as the Body of that Christ who has already, at terrible, at total cost to himself, bridged that gap by living the Kingdom in a world of sin; then the tension and the longing can begin to occasion not despair but determination, self-offering, joy even, as we continue along the pilgrim way. As Pablo Galdamez puts its, describing the reawakening Gospel in the slums of San Salvador:

When a people have stopped blaming their misfortunes on something outside themselves, and start organizing to fight

the causes of their own wretchedness, the good news of
Jesus has dawned on their horizon.[20]

That is why we receive God's Absolution. Of course it
doesn't suddenly make us sinless, of course it doesn't turn us
from publicans into Pharisees ('now at last I can leave sin –
and sinners – behind'); but it does take away the *sting* of sin,
so that – instead of being mastered by it, and bogged down
in a morass of despair and guilt at our own inadequacy and
the appalling state of the world – now at last, though still
utterly involved in sin (as Jesus was, more and more, right
up to his death), we can cast off the guilt and despair, and
use the tension and longing which remain as a springboard,
to become in our turn sin-bearers, sin-transformers, in the
image of the Lamb of God, signs of hope and forgiveness.

Forgive us, Father; hear our prayer.
We would walk with you anywhere,
through your suffering, with forgiveness,
take your life into the world.
Kyrie eleison, Christe eleison, Kyrie eleison.[21]

1 Mark 1:15; Matthew 4:17.
2 Baptism traditionally reflects both these Old Testament
stories of miraculous crossings (Exodus 14:21–22 and Joshua
3:14–17), though the Anglican Alternative Service Book
seems to have conflated them and done away with the
wilderness in the process: 'We thank you that through the
waters of the Red Sea you led your people out of slavery to
freedom in the promised land' (p. 246).
3 Lewis Carroll, *Alice in Wonderland*, passim.
4 Thomas Hardy, *Jude the Obscure*, part VI, §2.
5 Psalm 51(50):7–10 (RSV, adapted).
6 Luke 18:9–14.
7 I don't know the origin of this ditty, but I had it from the
late Fr Hugh Maycock.
8 'But for the grace of God, there goes John Bradford,'
observed John Bradford on seeing some criminals being led
to execution in the sixteenth century. (*Penguin Dictionary of
Quotations*, ed. J. M. and M. J. Cohen, 1960, p. 64).

9   See John 1:29.
10 See Hebrews 4:14–5, 10, etc.
11 2 Corinthians 5:21.
12 See *The Great Divorce*, Fontana 1972, pp. 110–111.
13 E.g. 19:3. We might be a little less keen on using the canticles from Revelation if we considered their context.
14 Christopher Burney, *Descent from Ararat.*
15 C. S. Lewis, *The Lion, the Witch, and the Wardrobe*, ch. 13 and ch. 15.
16 1 John 3:2.
17 Hebrews 5:7.
18 Alan Garner, *The Owl Service* (Collins 1967), ch. 27.
19 From '*Kyrie eleison*' by Jodi Page Clarke, in *Songs of the Spirit*, vol. 2 (Kevin Mayhew 1981), no. 197.
20 Pablo Galdamez (pseudonym of a European priest who worked in El Salvador from 1970 to 1980), *Faith of a People* (Orbis Books 1986), p. 24.
21 From Clarke, '*Kyrie eleison*'.

3

Gloria
The Wonder of the World

After penitence, the glory of God. The Eucharist follows the
pattern of Christ's life, of the Church's year. It begins with
an 'Advent' section, the call to repentance as we prepare for
Christ's coming. And now Christmas, the song of the angels
in the Bethlehem sky:

Glory in the highest to God,
and on earth peace, among people (of) good favour;[1]

and onwards from St Luke's original into that psalm of praise
which sprang up somewhere in the early Church and has now
become the most generally used non-biblical text of the whole
Christian world.

The origin of the rest of the hymn is unknown; even these
first two lines are obscure enough. Nobody knows if those
much-sung shepherds really did hear angels singing so long
ago, and walk in beneath the bright Palestinian moon to a still
little Bethlehem and a cave as yet uncluttered with religious
devotion and tourists, to offer their lambs and their wonder
to the newborn Christ. But the experience which Luke's story
describes, and which we recapture whenever we join in the
singing of glory to God: that is certain enough.

It is impossible to write adequately, or even at all, about
God's glory, which is, by definition, beyond definition: as St
Thomas Aquinas increasingly came to realize.[2] Ezekiel has a
try at it in the first chapter of his prophecy, but he only just
avoids being ridiculous, and in any case has to admit, at the
end of the chapter, that all he has actually described is 'the

appearance of the likeness of the glory of God':[3] words couldn't
get any nearer than that. And, even if they could; even if the
vision of glory could be encompassed by human writing; still
we couldn't write it, because we are not allowed, or not able,
ever, or at least in this life, to see the fullness of God's glory.
Moses asked, but was allowed only a back view:

> You cannot see my face; for man shall not see me and live.
> Behold, there is a place by me where you shall stand upon
>   the rock;
> and while my glory passes by I will put you in a cleft of
>   the rock,
> and I will cover you with my hand until I have passed by;
> then I will take away my hand, and you shall see my back;
> but my face shall not be seen.[4]

And, unlike Ezekiel, this writer makes no attempt to tell us
what sort of thing Moses did see. While the disciples, just
when they seemed to be getting near to it at the Transfiguration, fell asleep.[5]

We aren't given a direct view of God's glory, nor can it be
directly described. It appears to us only in snatches, whiffs,
glimpses, echoes, hints, shadows and fragments; it only
appears at all to those who are seeking it with all their heart,
and then it's generally when they aren't looking for it, when
they're looking the other way. Earlier on, Moses saw the
burning bush out of the corner of his eye; he had to 'turn
aside' from the way he thought he was going, to encounter
the holiness of God.[6]

Yet the experience of God's glory was a persistent one
for his people as they made their tortuous way through his
wilderness. It appeared 'by day in a pillar of cloud, and by
night in a pillar of fire' – which is a useful parable of how
God reveals himself to those who are seeking him. By day;
when the way is clear and straight, and the questions have
answers; then he appears as cloud, as mystery, as the one who
bewilders and befogs and blinds, as he bewildered Balaam on
his way to Moab,[8] as he blinded Saul on the Damascus road.[9]
But then, as we enter the mystery, the cloud, the darkness,
and discover that nothing at all is really known or clear; as

we get so overwhelmed by the chaos and ambiguity of life
that we look like sinking altogether into the slough; then at
last, as for Job in the whirlwind,[10] he appears in the pillar of
fire, not, indeed, with easy answers or clearcut systematic
theology, but offering, like the albatross, a living way forward
through the doubt and sorrow, though it is a way which costs
him and us not less than everything.

This elusive experience of the glory of God is a rare common
factor in the great diversity of the world's religions, though
it is portrayed in wildly different ways; from the heads of
Easter Island to the spire of Salisbury Cathedral, from many-
armed, animal-headed Hindu deities to the beckoning empti-
ness of the Islamic Mihrab, from the gaudiest, baroquest altar
to the simplest Meeting House.

One common image for the glory of God, which crops up
again and again in the Bible, is the appearance of angels. Are
there really such beings? The very question seems too prosaic,
like asking whether grace or beauty or wonder actually exist
. . . but we could say, at least, that the idea of angels gives
shape to what is beyond space, puts the inexpressible into at
least vaguely human terms. You can't tie angels down: Jacob
had a try, and received a lifelong wound for his pains[11] –
never mind what happened to the inhabitants of Sodom.[12]
Often, indeed, it isn't clear whether we are dealing directly
with God, or with his angel: as in the story of the Three Men
who came to Abraham and Sarah,[13] as in the incident of
the burning bush.[6] And it doesn't really make very much
difference, for how else could God, who is pure Spirit, ever
speak to material humanity, except through at least the sem-
blance of what is also material?

If we do accord an actual existence to angels, it would
certainly seem – at least in our terms – a much more provisional and dependent existence than that of the solid world
of matter. God can conjure angels up from wind and fire,
according to Psalm 104(103):4; and, according to the mis-
translation of that verse in the Epistle to the Hebrews,[14] he
can return them to their elements just as easily. In fact, he
can probably make them out of any material: any part of his

34

creation can blaze up, can be transfigured with his glory – a bush, a mountain, a person, a starlit sky, a field, a housing estate, a bus queue, a waterpot.

But, if the blaze is to become true fire, it needs an answering flare from the heart of the beholder. We rarely see angels: not because they aren't there, but because we are not attuned to them, we do not attend to them, we are too preoccupied with a more mundane wavelength. I once met a woman in a London park who, after going on at some length about the beauty of what lay around, ended her remarks with the memorable sentence: 'It is important to be thrilled by all this.' We need to cultivate the seed of glory sown at our birth – a theme dear to the Romantic poets, like Wordsworth in his *Intimations of Immortality*, or Lermontov:

An angel flew through the midnight sky,
And a gentle song he sang;
And the moon, and the stars, and the company of clouds
Listened to that holy song.
He sang of the bliss of sinless souls
Under the tents of heavenly gardens;
Of God in his greatness he sang,
And his praise was unfeigned.
In his arms he carried a young soul,
For the world of grief and tears,
And within that young soul the sound of his song
Remained without words, but alive.
And it languished long in the world,
Full of wonderful longing,
And the sounds of heaven could not be erased
Within it by the dull songs of earth.[15]

A major concern of the people of God should be to 'remember' the glory of God in our souls, to develop an awareness of angels – a process technically known as contemplation. If we aren't ready for the angels, they may very well pass by every twenty minutes, but we shall never see or hear them. For Christians, the archetypal contemplative is Mary, traditionally portrayed in icons with large, wide eyes, always open to the wonder of things; but with a small mouth, keeping the necessary silence. So she was ready for Gabriel when he came, responding with astonishment but with utter attuned-ness to the will of God.[16]

In Jesus, too, we find a soul completely attuned to the glory of God, so that he could perceive the inner life and sacred meaning of all those things, lives, and events around him which others would have called meaningless. In so much of his teaching – certainly in the parables – he looks right through the apparent ordinariness of judges at gates, fig trees and mustard trees, vineyards and those who work there, inci-dents in the family, at court, and along the road, and seeing – not *behind* them, as if they themselves had no significance; but *within* them, so lending them a new, deep and proper significance – an eternal meaning, a glimpse of God, the angels ascending and descending:

A man that looks on glass,
On it may stay his eye,
Or, if he pleaseth, through it pass,
And then the heaven espy.[17]

Sometimes, indeed, the 'espial' of heaven comes upon us in spite of ourselves, from an experience of great beauty, like Gerhard's vision of the night sky:

. . . and man, the marvel seeing,
forgets his selfish being,
   for joy of beauty not his own.
His care he drowneth yonder,
lost in the abyss of wonder;
   to heaven his soul doth steal . . .[18]

But in general it does not just happen 'if we please'; to see heaven and the angels is not a matter of whim, it requires a radical re-ordering of our life, and a willingness both to 'lose ourselves' in contemplation and to *let go* of the object of our contemplation. We can never enjoy something for what it is if we are grasping it to ourselves.

This may be part of the meaning of that strange beatitude 'Blessed are the meek, for they shall inherit the earth.'[19] At one level this is such obvious nonsense: the meek are, almost by definition, those who have the earth snatched away from them, like the aboriginal peoples of America and Australia. But, in fact, those who ostensibly 'possess' the earth are too snarled up by the thorns of possessiveness truly to 'inherit' it; and it is those who have 'plenty of nothing', those with empty hands and time to look, who can really enjoy the astonishing glory of God's world. St Francis only truly awoke to the glory of God in creation when he had stopped owning things, let go of everything, and begun living for God's glory alone, like the man who gave up everything for the Pearl of Great Price.[20] Mostly we are far too busy and bustling and self-important and possessive for that kind of thing.

This is surely what Jesus is complaining about in that perplexing passage between the parable of the Sower and its interpretation (Mark 4:11–12):

> To you has been given the mystery of the Kingdom of God, but to those outside everything happens in parables, so that
> 'seeing they may see and not perceive, and
> hearing they may hear and not take it in,
> lest they should turn again and it should be forgiven them'.

The contrast can't really be between those who are (unfairly) given the 'neat' truth about the Kingdom, and those who have to be content with theological cryptograms, for the simple reason that Jesus' parables are not cryptograms. The contrast, as in the verse about the man who looks on glass, is between those who merely see and those who perceive; those who merely hear and those who understand; those who can begin to fathom the mystery and those who remain on the surface, 'outside'. The challenge, as in verse 9 of the same passage, is to use our ears for their proper purpose: to hear the angels sing.

The true moment of glory arises when the spark of God's glory, hidden 'among the stuff' of his creation, discovers an answering spark in the depths of our soul, and the two leap up together in a single flame of adoration; or, in angelic terms, when we hear the song of the angels and are able to respond, to join in their singing. 'Glory' is a characteristic of God, and also our response to him: we see his glory, we give him glory. But the true *experience* of glory comes in the fusion of the two, it is the moment of encounter and reconciliation between two apparently separate things, when the spark leaps from one to the other and back again, and the differences melt away and the underlying unity of all things is revealed. So we experience glory not only at 'religious' moments, but at any 'moment of truth': when we perceive a pattern in things for the first time; when everything suddenly 'makes sense'; when a piece of music, or a painting, or a place, speaks directly to our soul; when we fall in love. All such moments of 'cosmic disclosure', as Bishop Ian Ramsey put it,[21] are a potential source of conversion, of new life and inspiration, whether we choose to frame them in theological language or not; whether our response is 'Glory be!' or something less pious.

This flaring up of glory, this encounter between God and Man, is sometimes – so tradition has it – so strong that it can actually be seen from outside, objectively. Moses had to cover his face with a veil after communing with God, to prevent the Israelites from being dazzled. The great saints are said to have shone with an aura of radiance, stylized in Christian art as the halo. Indeed, some of our contemporary 'saints' do seem indefinably to *shine*, and many of us will have met people who could properly be described as 'radiant'; temporarily, as a result of some 'moment of glory' as outlined above, or more permanently after years of seeking God's face in prayer and holiness.

And in the story of Jesus, who communed with God in a continuous flow of responsive love, glory flares out again and again; at the moments of Epiphany – the shining of the star, the presentation in the Temple, the baptism, the marriage at Cana, and of course the Transfiguration; and, in St John's account, throughout the story and above all at those moments when he pronounces the *I AM*, a saying so powerful that it even sends the soldiers who have come to arrest him staggering back on to the ground.[22] And, as in the glory of creation, so in the life of Jesus the glory that is revealed is more than we can possibly take in or encompass: at Cana he makes *far* more wine than the best of human parties could conceivably have needed;[23] at Bethsaida there was too much bread even for thousands of people.[24]

To be the vehicle of the glory of God is essential to being the Son of God, to being truly human. So it was for Jesus, and so it is to be for us:

> All of us, with unveiled face,
> mirroring the glory of the Lord,
> are being transformed in the same image [icon]
> from glory to glory,
> as from the Lord, the Spirit.[25]

So at the Eucharist, which is the anticipation of our coming humanity, Christhood, divinization, glorification; the celebration of God's glory is an essential element. We can't conjure it up, of course: but we can rehearse the experience of glory in our own lives, in the life of the Christian Church, and in the life of Christ; and we can express our hope of the glory to be revealed. And if we do this faithfully with all our hearts, sooner or later we shall encounter God's glory here as well.

Therefore it is important that we should consciously sing with the angels: here, in the first part of the service (Gloria in excelsis); later, as we open ourselves to the glory of the Gospel ('Alleluia'); and, later still, as we approach the heart of the mystery and relive the awe of Isaiah ('Holy, holy, holy').[26] The eucharistic preface in the *Liturgy of St James* well conveys this awe, conveys also the sheer inability of mere words to bear such a weight of glory:

> It is indeed meet and right, fitting and necessary,
> to praise thee, to sing to thee, to bow down to thee, to glorify thee, to thank thee,
> the Creator of every visible and invisible creature,
> the treasury of eternal good, the source of life and immortality,
> the God and Master of everything,

whom the heavens and the highest heavens sing
   and all their powers,
the sun and moon, the whole choir of stars,
the earth, the sea, and all that is in them,
the heavenly Jerusalem, the gathering of the elect,
   the Church of the first-born,
those enrolled in the heavens,
   the spirits of the just and the prophets,
   the souls of the martyrs and apostles,
the angels, archangels, thrones, dominations, principalities,
   and virtues, and the fearsome powers;
the many-eyed Cherubim, and the six-winged Seraphim,
who with two wings cover their faces, with two their feet,
   and with two they fly,
and call out one to another
   with tireless lips and unsilenced doxologies
singing the triumphal hymn of thy magnificent glory,
   with clear voices
shouting, glorifying, crying aloud, and saying:
   HOLY, HOLY, HOLY . . .[27]

All our singing should have at least a mildly angelic flavour;
or, rather, it is the function of our singing to bring out the
glorious, angelic, heavenly quality of the Eucharist as a whole.
Songs, hymns, anthems, choruses and the rest should not be
additional elements in the service, extra items on the pro-
gramme ('now we'll stop for a moment and sing a hymn'):
they should pervade and inform the whole liturgy, not interrupting but deepening its flow and rhythm – so that, in the
traditional Catholic order of Mass, every song is ascribed to
a moment when something else is happening: as the ministers
enter, as the Gospel is prepared, as the offertory is brought
up, and so on. In the Tridentine Mass, indeed, as in the
Orthodox Liturgy, much of the singing actually goes on at
the same time as the priest is saying other prayers; which
may seem an absurdity, an abuse even, to our tidy Western
minds, but which can feel like a blazing up of glory: what is
being spoken and prayed about is too wonderful to be contained in mere words, it has to be accompanied by the singing

of people and angels. It is as if the singing lent colour and light to the insufficient black-and-whiteness of the spoken word, like the illumination and decoration of a Book of Hours.

Perhaps the most exuberantly angelic liturgy of the entire Church is that of the Ethiopians, where the words of standard prayers continually flare out in extraordinary directions, as in this blessing:

O ye Christian people,
as ye have gathered together on this day,
so also may he gather you on the holy Mount of Zion
    and in the free Jerusalem in heaven,
and as ye have heard the voice of Mary's praise,
so may he suffer you to hear the word of the infants' harps
and the angels' song, which softens even the very bones
    because of the multitude of its melodies.
May he lead you where there are stretched out
    the tabernacles of the flaming fire wherein the High
        Priest is
    and wherein are the pictured appearance of his face,
    the pure and bright dress which the hand of man did
        not make,
    but it was woven above.
May he lead you to where are
    the congregation of the holy prophets,
    the congregation of the preaching apostles,
    the congregation of the victorious martyrs,
    the congregation of the blessed righteous,
    the congregation of the ordained priests,
    the congregation of the watchful angels,
    and the congregation of virgins and perfect monks,
with all the perfect congregations of the One Holy
        Universal Church,
and with them where there is the Ark of the Wilderness,
    our Lady Mary . . .[28]

The words are extravagant enough; but this Liturgy does not seem to consist primarily of words at all, but of song: an unending weaving of otherworldly harmonies for almost all

# #

the two or more hours of the service, charging the already outlandish words with unmistakable glory and wonder.

This colourful, heavenly exuberance, which so strongly marks the liturgies of the Eastern churches (and is found also in much Pentecostal worship), is too often dolefully absent from the reformed churches in the 'middle' of the spectrum, post-Vatican II Catholicism as well as mainline Protestantism. We have become intolerably cerebral and wordy and orderly and logical; the microphone, that enemy of mystery, has replaced the censer as the vital adjunct to all worship; and, whereas in the East the 'said Mass' does not exist, here in the West its creeping matter-of-factness has taken over even our Sunday worship.

This is not a plea for obscurantism, rather for keeping alive in our Christian worship those vital elements of mystery, awe, silence and song which the world around is so unhappily losing: if we lose them too, what a betrayal of our world that would be, for we are the world's guardians of song and wonder. In a world where fewer and fewer people sing to themselves, where nothing is considered worthwhile unless it is functional, we should beware of also minimalizing our liturgy, of the attitude which seeks to pare away everything except the bare bones that keep it 'valid'; for our aim is not 'validity', but the glorification of mankind, the meeting of heaven and earth in the cloud and the fire.

Our Eucharist should express our calling to divinization, and awaken the embers of glory in our soul to the breathing of the glory of God – in heaven, in creation, in the world, in history, in the community, in others, and in our own being. The singing together of 'psalms, hymns and spiritual songs'[29] is a vital way of attuning ourselves with the song and wonder of the angels, and the *Gloria in Excelsis* sets the tone for the whole service.

However, the *Gloria* does not stop with the first phrase. It goes off first into an Ethiopian-style explosion of wonder:

We praise thee, we bless thee, we worship thee, we glorify thee,
We give thanks to thee for thy great glory . . .

42

But a new note, already foreshadowed by the promise of peace on earth, is struck in the second paragraph, with its reprise of the *Kyrie eleison* motif:

> O Lord God, Lamb of God, Son of the Father,
> that takest away the sins of the world,
> have mercy upon us . . .

We may be able to catch and celebrate odd hints of heavenly glory now, but these are very much a foretaste of what lies ahead: once again, we have not yet reached the Promised Land. The peace of God's Kingdom is not yet. And, until it comes, there must always be a strong element of pain, of unease, in the song we sing; for both the times when we may experience 'disclosure', and the times when glory seems a remote concept and we feel only deadness, awaken not satisfaction but an intolerable longing in the soul. We should sing, we need to sing; but our singing can never be merely jolly. It has always been painful to 'sing the Lord's song in a strange land';[30] a considerable portion of our *Gloria* needs to be in the minor key.

It *is* painful to sing 'peace on earth' in a world like ours; if we sing it with our hearts, we shall be wounded by the contrast between this peace which we sing, for which we long, and the terrible unpeacefulness that surrounds and invades us. But to sing 'peace on earth' is not just to express a wild hope or a vain longing: our song must in the end spill over from liturgy into life, so that our life itself in turn becomes a song of peace – and that will always be a hard song to sing.

For our Christian life, like the life of Jesus, is set between the song of the angels and the cross of the world's grimness; a tension that issues equally in pain and singing, as we hear so clearly in musical traditions like the Negro spiritual and the harmonies of the Russian Church. It would be so much easier to let go of one pole or other: to forget God's glory and accept the grain of the world, or to concentrate gnostically on the 'spiritual' realms, letting 'the things of the world grow strangely dim'. But we must hold on to both, allowing the current of pain and glory to flow through us and out in almost unbearable melody: living and singing the tension between the sinful world and the song of its Creator.

How can we sing the Lord's song in a strange land? How can we sing 'peace on earth' in a warring world? How can we sing Magnificat in a world of such injustice? How can we sing Benedictus, with its confidence in God's lordship over history, in a world where history seems to be leading nowhere? How can we sing Benedicite, the song of the glory of creation, when that creation is being polluted and torn apart? How can we sing Nunc Dimittis, such peaceful calm at the end of the day, when our nights are full of nightshifts and nightmares and restlessness and a relentless orange glow; when our lives are as likely to end in disintegration, loneliness and frustration, as in fulfilment and peace? Simeon could depart in peace, but so many are more like Peter, stretching out our hands and being girded by others and being carried where we have no wish to go.[31] And what of the end of mankind, and of the world? We sing – as I have written – of eschatological hope, of a coming divinization, of the consummation of all things in the glory of the Trinity; but futurologists do not generally bear this out, pointing instead to disintegration, entropy and annihilation.

Yet, somehow, we must sing on; for the *Gloria* of our lips and our lives reflects not only the beauties of a distant heaven, but God's creative power now; it is not only a song, but a pledge; not only a prophecy, but an embodiment of that prophecy, for a world that sings will be a world redeemed. 'Doxology', the giving of glory, is the purpose of our worship, but also of mankind: and true liturgy, liturgy that looks outwards and embraces mankind, will bring that glorification one step nearer to fulfilment.

1   Luke 2:13–14. There are two possible readings, and three possible interpretations, of the last phrase; 'on earth peace among people of goodwill'; 'on earth peace among people who are in (presumably God's) good favour'; or 'on earth peace, goodwill among people'.
2   Towards the end of his life the great systematic theologian is

supposed to have said 'Such things have been revealed to me that what I have written seems but straw.'

3 Ezekiel 1:28.
4 Exodus 33:20–33.
5 Luke 9:33. Admittedly 'when they woke up, they saw his glory'; but it sounds from verse 33 as if they hadn't really come round.
6 Exodus 3:1–6.
7 Exodus 13:21–22.
8 Numbers 22:21–35.
9 Acts 9:3–8.
10 Job 38:1ff.
11 Genesis 32:24–31.
12 Genesis 19:1–25.
13 Genesis 18:1ff.
14 Hebrews 1:7.
15 M. Lermontov, 'The Angel', Oxford Book of Russian Verse (OUP 1925), no. 74 (my translation).
16 Luke 1:34–38.
17 George Herbert, 'The Elixir', from *The Temple* (1633).
18 From the Yattendon translation of '*Nun ruhen alle Wälder*' by P. Gerhardt, no. 34 in *Hymns Ancient and Modern Revised*.
19 Matthew 5:5.
20 Matthew 13:45–46.
21 During his mission to Oxford University in 1969.
22 John 18:5–6. Jesus' reply to the soldiers, which loses a great deal in translation, is in fact simply I AM; cf. John 4:26, 6:20, 8:58 and, most surprisingly, Mark 14:62 – as well as the more obvious instances at John 6:35, 8:12, 10:7, 10:11, 11:25, 14:6 and 15:1.
23 John 2:6–11.
24 Mark 6:35–44 and parallels.
25 2 Corinthians 3:18.
26 Isaiah 6:3.
27 The *Liturgy of St James*, Brotherhood of St Mark of Ephesus (1978), p. 25.
28 The Ethiopian *Qaddase*, translated by Sister Abraham (unpublished).
29 Ephesians 5:19; Colossians 3:16.
30 Psalm 137(136):4.
31 John 21:18.

4

Word
Poetry and Response

For a stranger in church, the first bit of the Eucharist may be rather bewildering. A good deal of singing, to which she may not be accustomed (and even if she is, she probably won't know the tunes). Strange people around; a book that seems impossible to follow; and a general uncertainty about what is going on, worse if the *Kyries* are sung in Greek, or the *Gloria* to one of those tunes that swallows up half a sentence in one bar of music.

But now a reassuring moment: breath is taken, throats are cleared, chairs scraped; the ritual grinds to a halt, and at last (as long as the translation is lucid, the reader is audible, and the microphone is working) here comes something apparently straightforward: the reading of Scripture. *This is the Word of the Lord!* for us all to mark, learn and inwardly digest; straight talk from on high; marching orders for the week ahead.

That is what many are longing for. From the beginning, people have sought a definitive Word from the Lord that will finally answer the needs and questions of humanity; and more than one of the world religions is based on such a Word: Judaism on the revelation to Moses, Islam on that to Mohammed, Mormonism on that to Joseph Smith. I once asked a Moslem a rather facetious question about the observance of Ramadan in Lapland, and he answered, without batting an eyelid, 'I don't know, but it will tell you somewhere in the Koran'. God has spoken once for all, and we know where we are with him.

And they sought such a Word from Jesus. After his long

46

period of preparation – thirty years of 'hidden life', forty days of prayer and fasting – he 'came into Galilee proclaiming God's good news';[1] according to Luke, 'he began to teach in their synagogues, and was given glory by all . . . and they were astonished at his teaching, because his word was with authority'.[2] The first chapters of Mark's Gospel convey a breathless excitement about this ministry of the Word; here was something new, powerful, God-given; so it is not surprising that people looked to him for the definite answer to all manner of questions: on the purposes of God, the Kingdom of heaven, the future of the nation, the problem of suffering, the end of time, and his own person and mission.

But straight answers were not forthcoming. Not that the questions weren't dealt with; but the result was never a comfortable answer, usually rather an unnerving challenge and a throwing back of the question. The 'rich young ruler' asked about salvation, expecting an answer in terms of law, but was given one about lifestyle;[3] the lawyer wanted a neat definition of 'neighbour', and got the highly disconcerting story of the Good Samaritan;[4] those seeking a reassuring sign were given only Jonah;[5] Pilate asked who Jesus was and received only silence.[6] You can get badges and car stickers proclaiming 'Jesus is the Answer'; but, if so, he was and is a very disconcerting answer. 'Jesus is the Question' might be closer to the gospel picture. He taught not in cold facts but in stories, signs, pictures; in poetry, not in prose.

Jesus didn't give easy answers; so it would be a mistake, and untrue to him, to look for them in the liturgical 'Ministry of the Word', the reading of the Bible, which is one way he addresses us today. It is too often supposed that a 'literal' interpretation of the Bible is the only one that does it full justice; that to be 'biblical' means to be a fundamentalist. Whereas, on the contrary, it is the fundamentalist approach, treating the Bible like a spiritual railway timetable, which does the greatest violence to its true nature.

The Bible is an anthology of very diverse writings, spanning at least 1,000 years of history, and written by all sorts of people for all sorts of different reasons: so one couldn't possibly expect it to be uniformly accurate, consistent, or even relevant. It is not at all surprising, for example, that the author of Psalm 37 had quite different ideas about human suffering from the writer of Job; that the creation stories in Genesis 1 and 2 do not tally; or that the various New Testament writers have differing memories and interpretations of the life of Jesus. Such 'inconsistency' is treated as a weakness, both by the attackers of Christianity and by those Christians who misguidedly try to sweep it away: but, on the contrary, it is precisely this diversity that gives the Bible its richness and its strength.

To pretend that the Bible is always accurate is not only to miss the point, it can also be dangerous. For within its pages there are sharply differing views of God and the way he wants us to behave; much damage has been done – and is still being done – by taking them all literally. Did the Lord really meet Moses and try to kill him as he was on his way to Pharaoh – and only leave him alone because Zipporah cut off her son's foreskin and touched Moses' feet with it?[7] Are we really to admire the way the Israelites butchered their way into the Promised Land (with all its connotations for the situation there today?)[8] Are we really to join the saints of Revelation as they joyfully contemplate the smoke of their enemies rising to heaven for ever and ever?[9] The Bible is not always morally or theologically reliable, for it charts the moral and theological *development* of a people: and fundamentalism, which ignores this, can justify all kinds of horrors in the name of a 'God of the Bible' who is far removed from the God and Father of our Lord Jesus Christ.

The Bible is not uniformly reliable and pure; and, whether they admit it or not, Christians have always picked and chosen. Individuals underline the texts they like; printers highlight the inspiring bits, or put the uninspiring bits in smaller print; churches provide lectionaries that leave out the irrelevant, nasty, or naughty bits (even the magnificently comprehensive Anglican lectionary of 1662 cuts out a lot of Leviticus and most of Ezekiel).

Inevitably, too, what the Bible says depends on how it is interpreted. Scripture doesn't just speak for itself; we all interpret it in our own way, and those who pour scorn on the subtler interpretations of biblical scholarship are usually only doing so to make way for the grosser interpretations of fundamentalism. What is the 'plain meaning' of the Passover story,[10] the Sixth Commandment,[11] the servant songs in Isaiah,[12] the Parable of the Unjust Steward,[13] the Epistle to the Romans, and the apocalypses of the Gospels[14] and Revelation? Everyone's answer will depend on their culture, their historical background, their temperament, their interests and the degree of their prejudice.

What is more, every translation is itself also an interpretation: there is no such thing (as Muslims rightly affirm) as a 'straight' translation. Two translators can give the same passage an entirely different meaning or nuance; and so much depends on how it is read, where the emphasis is put, where the reading begins and ends, and how it is combined with other passages from Scripture or elsewhere. By the time it reaches our ears in church, the Bible has been subjected to as much processing and packaging as potato crisps; it is hard to affirm that this is God's Word straight.

For Muslims, the untidiness of the Bible is a clear pointer to the decadence of Christianity. Originally, they maintain, there was one, pure, unambiguous Gospel revealed to the prophet Jesus (peace be upon him); but the early Church lost it, and can now only provide four confusing and conflicting secondary accounts: a sorry contrast to the monolithic purity and heaven-sent clarity of the Koran.

But our Bible is not to be compared with the Koran. For Muslims, the Koran is the ultimate revelation of God's Word, and Mohammed, the last and greatest of the prophets, was sent to reveal it: whereas for Christians it is *Jesus Christ* who is the ultimate Word of God, and the Bible which reveals *him*. So it is not surprising if it is a very different sort of document.

An illustration of the difference between the two religions, and the nature of their Scriptures, could be made from their two great shrines in the Old City of Jerusalem. The Muslim Dome of the Rock towers above the city, a superbly pure, graceful, homogeneous building, decorated with perfect geometrical designs; devout and united prayer is offered, in harmony with every other mosque throughout the world, five times a day. The Christian Church of the Holy Sepulchre – if you manage to find it at all – is a vast, ill-kept and bewildering jumble of different architectural styles and periods, all on different levels, and divided up between six different denominations who often celebrate their arcane, loud and incompatible liturgies simultaneously and in competition, if not open conflict, with one another.

Which hardly puts Christianity in an attractive light. But the Church of the Holy Sepulchre has one huge hidden strength: it is all-embracing. It reflects all the richness – and all the grime – of Christian history, even of humanity itself. It is, for the sinner, a more comfortable place to be. And the Bible is the same: it reflects our admirable and also our disgraceful qualities. It doesn't obscure the difficulties of being human, or of belief in God. It shows us many noble figures, but does not skirt round their ignoble qualities. We are allowed to see the disobedience of Adam and Eve, the drunkenness of Noah, the duplicity of Jacob, the faithlessness of Moses, the callous adultery of David, the hotheadedness of Peter, the intolerance of Paul, and yes, even the anger and frustratedness of Jesus himself. And the Bible itself can also display such all too human characteristics: anger, self-righteousness, incomprehension, obscurity, unreliability, limited vision. Which makes it less beautiful and less clear; but, easier to feel at home with, which is what really matters. We may choke over the curses in Psalm 109; but what a solace to Gonville ffrench-Beytagh, when the lectionary allowed him to say them during his solitary confinement in a South African jail.[15]

Whoever sits down for the Ministry of the Word expecting the Plain Truth will be disappointed. The Bible is not a neat archive of plain truth or clean living, but an extraordinary jumbled attic, full of all our Christian furniture and curios and long-lost treasures, and things that nobody can remember whom they belonged to or what they are for. Some are obviously valuable, some are pretty worthless, some are cheap but of sentimental importance, some don't look much but may prove priceless if we examine them properly. Some bits we regularly dust down and put on display, others – sometimes rightly, sometimes wrongly – are generally left under wraps.

All this may seem a profane description of sacred Scripture. But our Scriptures are not sacred from any objective superiority: because they were dictated by God, and are therefore *a priori* more glorious and reliable than anything else ever written; or because they are manifestly the most beautiful or profound or spiritual writings ever produced (though many of them do have those qualities.) They are sacred to us because of their intimate and unique connection with Jesus Christ, and with the Church which first proclaimed him. The Old Testament was Jesus' Bible, so is vital for our understanding of his vocation and mission; the New Testament draws together the earliest witnesses to his life and its meaning. Even here, of course, the corners are not smoothly rounded: our 'canon' of Scripture was not settled for centuries, and some of the eventual decisions about which books should be put in or left out now seem arbitrary, even bizarre. But this witnesses to the continuity of life between Jesus and his Church: the Bible is the Church's book, and, if the Church made some arbitrary decisions, well, that is only an extension of the arbitrary background of Jesus himself. The 'scandal of particularity' in Jesus is continued in his Bible and his Church.

The Bible is the Church's book, handed on from one generation to the next, and linking us now (as the Eucharist does) with our fellow-Christians across the world and down the ages. But it isn't just a relic, depending for its power upon a 2,000-year-old link with the historical Jesus; like all holy things, it gives us an inescapable sense of being grasped by something greater and stronger than ourselves, that the living Christ is using Scripture to address us now.

The reading of Scripture must be a living experience. We are not dealing with texts that are 'true' but dead. Their 'truth' is a living truth. In some cases this will include factual or historical truth: in others 'literal' truth is a meaningless concept. Are the Psalms literally true? Or the Parables? Obviously not: but that doesn't prevent their being powerful vehicles of God's Word for us. And there are many other parts of Scripture whose literal truth is largely irrelevant. The story of Job may conceivably be based on something that once happened: but what matters is not whether it happened, but the questions of suffering and evil which it raises. Jesus may or may not have been born of a virgin, turned water into wine, walked on the lake, done instantaneous healings, spoken of himself as the Son of God, and walked through walls after his death: despite all the labour and ink that has been spent on these subjects, we can never find out, we can only surmise according to our own particular, and most likely arbitrary, way of thinking and feeling.

The historical questions are interesting, even important, but secondary. What matters for us about the life of Jesus – as for the evangelists, St Paul and the other New Testament writers – is not its historical detail but its present and lasting significance. St Luke wrote his birth narratives for the same reason as St John wrote his preface: to tell us who Jesus was and what his life meant. The stories of miracles always point beyond the event to the meaning; above all the stories of the resurrection, which show us that the life of Christ did not stop with the death of Jesus.

God speaks not through the prose and deadness of literalism – 'this is so, this is not so, for me and for everyone' – but through the poetry of imagination, excitement, infuriation, enjoyment. As with all poetry, we have to open ourselves, our minds and our hearts, to what is being said, letting it work on us, letting ourselves be changed by it. Its truth is not the truth of an almanac, but the truth of purging fire; the truth of the Spirit who casts down and judges and creates and renews, the truth of Jesus Christ who left no one he met untouched.

The Ministry of the Word at the Eucharist is, or should be, a continuation of the Ministry of the Word made flesh: if God speaks to us through this part of the service, it is not because we have met the Bible, but the living Christ.

Jesus' ministry was never cosy or facile; he never gave in to immature demands; but he did meet the deepest longings of those around him, creating an immense gladness of body and soul. Here was the Word of which the psalmist sang:

How sweet are your words to my taste,
sweeter than honey to my mouth![16]

But this sweetness had the power to deliver; it was a 'teaching with authority',[17] as people soon came to recognize; like the description in Isaiah 55:

As the rain and the snow come down from heaven,
and return not thither but water the earth,
making it bring forth and sprout . . .
so shall my word be that goes forth from my mouth;
it shall not return to me empty,
but it shall accomplish that which I purpose,
and prosper in the thing for which I sent it.[19]

And, once it had sunk in, the teaching did not always seem so sweet; much of it was unpalatable to the establishment, like the prophecy of Revelation:

And I took the little scroll out of the angel's hand, and ate it up,
and it was in my mouth as sweet as honey;
and when I had eaten it, my stomach was made bitter.
And they said to me;
Again you must prophesy about peoples and nations and tongues and kings, many of them.[19]

A further description of God's Word is in the Letter to the Hebrews; that it is

living and active,
sharper than any two-edged sword,
piercing to the division of soul and spirit, of joints and marrow,
and discerning the thoughts and intentions of the heart.[20]

This certainly conveys the uncomfortable, challenging side of Jesus' ministry; but it also speaks of the immense sensitivity with which he was able to pronounce precisely the right word to each person, in every situation. He 'knew what was in Man';[21] with the delicacy of a surgeon, he could perceive the exact point in a person's soul to which the word of healing or forgiveness, criticism or challenge, had to be spoken if they were to grow into wholeness rather than sink into despair or complacency.

This often happens at the Ministry of the Word. When the reader says 'This is the Word of the Lord', at the end of each passage, we may quite often feel more like replying 'oh really?' or 'are you sure?' or even 'tell that to the marines' than the prescribed pious 'Thanks be to God'. But this is the ministry of *Christ* the Word: and, when we give thanks at the end of each reading, it is because we have received Christ – not passively, but in the interaction of our own spirit with that of the Scripture. With every reading, for every listener, this interaction will be different: just as it was in Galilee. We may hear God's Word through a deep sense of affinity with the reading: 'Yes, yes, *of course*, that is exactly what I've been groping towards'; or because it challenges us, as when St Anthony was driven into the desert by the story of the Rich Young Ruler; or because it makes us thoroughly indignant, (I remember a very articulate factory worker reacting furiously to the passage in Ecclesiasticus which says that artisans can't reflect);[22] or even through asking why it leaves us cold.

A 'Ministry of the Word' that is true to Jesus, then, is as likely to be a disturbing as a comforting experience; though the comfort is always there once he has managed to strip away the layers of falsehood and pretence with which we cover ourselves. But, however it affects us, the Word, 'alive and active', is made known through the vital meeting which takes place when Scripture, and particularly the Gospel, is read; a meeting between ourselves, the writer of the passage, his situation and ours, the things which the reading brings to our mind, and the Spirit of God informing the whole encounter.

Once again, the stories in the Bible are icons. They are an invitation to engage with the way, the truth, the life of God's Kingdom now; to enter now into the story of Christ. So if their effect on us is different from that on St Augustine, or Thomas Aquinas, or John Wesley, or on another Christian of a different tradition, never mind: it is only a sign of their power, their universality, their hardiness in so many different soils. What each receives will be unique and new; and we can extend the Ministry, as in Bible studies or Quaker meetings, by sharing what we have received: as long as no one tries to foist his insights on others for whom the message may be different.

The climax of this part of the service is the proclamation of the Gospel of Christ, its special character often emphasized by standing up, the singing of acclamations, processions, candles, incense, and so on. In the *Liturgy of St John Chrysostom*, for example, the reading of the Gospel is preceded by alleluias, the greeting of peace, the singing of glory, and this prayer:

> O Master who love mankind,
> make the spotless light of your divine wisdom
>   shine in our hearts,
> and open the eyes of our mind to an understanding
>   of the things you teach us in the Gospel.
> Instil in us a fear of your blessed commandments,
> so that, trampling upon the desires of the flesh,
> we may begin to lead a spiritual life,
> both thinking and doing all things according to your
>   pleasure.
> For you are the enlightenment of our souls and bodies,
>   Christ our God,
> and we give glory to you, together with your eternal Father
> and your all-holy, good, and life-giving Spirit,
> now and always and through the ages of ages. Amen.[23]

Then the deacon sings 'Let us attend!' Jesus spoke his Word all over the place; but, as in the story of the Sower, it was only certain people who were ready and able to receive it. If the living Word is to become 'alive and active' in our souls, we need to be receptive, to 'attend'; the 'eyes of our mind' must indeed be opened; we must, as Jesus said, 'have ears to hear'.

But the readings must also be allowed to *resonate* for us. Resonance matters. Even the structure and acoustics of the building matter. Arches, domes and soaring vaults may not make hearing any easier, but they do give a proper context of worship and of eternity; whereas in a low-ceilinged room with padded walls one may accurately hear every syllable, but in far too flat and mundane a fashion. The Ministry of the Word is a shared experience; the words need to echo around between us before they reach the individual ear. For the same reason it would be a pity if we altogether gave up singing, as well as speaking, the texts: and, when they are spoken, they need to be read with attention, and with a right balance between meaningless nonchalance and self-indulgent histrionic.

Resonant, too, should be the translation we use. Different styles of translation have different values: the theological student who doesn't know Hebrew will need something different from the new Christian who just wants to find out what sort of thing is there. What is needed in *worship* is a translation that conveys the flavour, and the resonance, and the *poetry* of the original, something which can stir the hearer like the psalmist's 'deep calling on deep'. Too many translators have ironed out the essential ambiguities, turning poetry into prose and leaving no space for doubt or imagination. The King James Version may well have wrong resonances, words like 'charity' that have changed their meaning, interpretations we now know to be wrong, and too much of a smell of Old England, pew rents, squires and an irrecoverable childhood; but so much modern translation has practically no resonance at all, fitting in too well with dull low-ceilinged buildings, nasal electronic organs, and prosaic unmysterious worship. Its language can be a terrible combination of the donnish and the banal: can we really imagine Jesus answering Mary 'Your concern, Mother, is not mine',[24] or the voice from heaven thundering 'On thee my favour rests'?[25]

There are two further ways for God's Word to resonate in the Eucharist. The first is through the *sermon*, which at its best will be integral to the Ministry of the Word, but as more than icing on the cake or froth on the beer. The sermon should be an opening up of the texts, not insisting on one interpretation at the expense of others, but offering new freedom of thought, new possibilities for understanding – and new challenges to life. As with Scripture itself, as later with the gifts of bread and wine, so God can take the preached word and speak through it, breathe fresh life into it, make Christ present in it. Here again, the Word is spoken uniquely to each listener: most preachers have had the experience of being warmly thanked – or upbraided – for something in a sermon that was never intended, or quite misunderstood, or taken out of context, or blown up out of all proportion. 'But *that* isn't what I was saying at all!' Maybe not; but maybe that is what God wants them to hear.

The sermon is an art form, weaving the texts together with the events of the week, the life of the Church, and whatever is on people's hearts at the moment. It is a priestly expression of where we are in our journey towards God, as well as an attempt to suggest the next step forward. And when this artistic endeavour – which, like the painting of icons, requires much prayerful attention – actually succeeds; then it can become not only an address by the preacher to the congregation, but an offering on their behalf: this is how it is for us now, God, given what you've been doing and saying to us. The preacher will know if this has happened from the response: from a sense of concentration; from that nodding of heads which means roughly the same as a Pentecostal 'Amen! Hallelujah!'; from the quality of the silence which follows.

For *silence* is the other means of resonance. Our world is a great clutter of words, mostly fairly meaningless – one cartoon shows a man holding up an umbrella to ward off the verbal downpour:[26] the Church and its liturgy must be an oasis from the verbiage, allowing the Word of Life to be heard. It is hard to hear God speaking, to distinguish 'the very Word of the Lord', if the Eucharist, too, is nothing but a stream of words. But how vividly the Word can stand out in the context of silence; silence is the necessary setting for the jewel, if the jewel is to be seen to its full advantage. Silence and spoken words can fertilize one another: the silence allowing the words to resonate, the words awakening, in the silence, that often voiceless Word which God speaks in our depths.

God's Word is not shut up in the Bible: he speaks, not from the sacred page or the silver screen, but in the interaction of Scripture – and often other writings too – with human experience. Listen again to Pablo Galdamez:

> The lectorate used to be the third step along the road to the priesthood. We too were lectors, readers, in the Salvadoran slums and ghettos.
>
> With God's word in hand, we tried to find answers to our problems, and we learned where to find the will of God so that we could keep moving ahead. That will was to be found in life, in our conscience . . . When this conscience, each one's conscience, starts interacting with other people's consciences collectively . . . you can read God's will. We also learned to read this will of God in the Bible. One who can read life can easily discover the key to Holy Scripture, with all those living stories of a people on its way to freedom. Another place to read the will of God is in the Christian community. In our group meetings we discovered trails leading to signs of God. And finally, in the poor . . .[27]

'This is the Word of the Lord: thanks be to God.' That isn't just stating how infallible it all is, but accepting whatever God is saying in our hearts and lives. More: like the *Amen* at Communion, it indicates a willingness, as individuals and as a body, to be shaped by Christ the living Word into his own likeness. The Word of the Lord has been transferred to us. As we celebrate the Word, we, like Jesus, actually *become* the Word: we don't just hear it, we soak it up and let it soak us up, till it becomes incarnate in us also. And, like Jesus, we aren't just to speak or preach, but to live, to *be* God's Word for the world: our life, the Church's life, will become a Ministry of the Word, even before we open our mouths.

The 'Gospel procession' is a sign that we can't keep Christ's Good News for ourselves; we *must* go out from here, singing what we have received. When Paul says 'It is woe for me if I don't preach the Gospel',[28] he doesn't mean 'I'll burn in

58

hell if I don't go around proselytizing', but 'the Gospel is so wonderful, it hurts to keep it in'. Like the Sower in the parable,[29] we are to spread the Word indiscriminately over all the fields and paths of God's creation, awakening in others the vibrations of hope it has set going in ourselves. And never mind the fowls of the air: they may always leave the seed further on, unknown to us, like the migratory birds who pick up acacia seeds in Tanzania and drop them in the Jordan valley, where they put down deep roots to unseen rivers, and flower in the autumn.

1   Mark 1:14.
2   Luke 4:15, 32.
3   Mark 10:17–22 and parallels.
4   Luke 10:25–37.
5   Luke 11:29–30, Matthew 12:38–40.
6   Mark 15:2–5.
7   Exodus 4:24–26.
8   See, for example, Joshua ch. 10.
9   Revelation 19:1–4.
10 Exodus 11:1—12:32. This story is laden with allegorical significance, but we could only feel disgust for a God who actually behaved in such a way. The Easter readings must be difficult for the Egyptian Church.
11 Exodus 20:13; Deuteronomy 5:17. Is this a pacifist's charter or isn't it?
12 In Isaiah 42, 49, 50, 52, and 53. Do these passages refer to the prophet, another individual, the people, or Jesus – or to more than one of these?
13 Luke 16:1–9. The 'plain meaning' of this parable certainly seems to have got lost somewhere along the line.
14 Mark 13; Matthew 24; Luke 17:22–37 and 21:5–36. Was Jesus talking about the fall of Jerusalem, the end of the world, or the events of the twentieth century?
15 The story of the imprisonment of Gonville ffrench-Beytagh when he was Dean of Johannesburg is told in his autobiographical *Encountering Darkness*. But this anecdote I heard in a talk.
16 Psalm 119(118):103 (RSV, adapted).

17   Mark 1:27.
18   Isaiah 55:11.
19   Revelation 10:10–11.
20   Hebrews 4:12.
21   John 2:25.
22   Ecclesiasticus (Ben Sirach) 38:24–34.
23   The *Liturgy of St John Chrysostom*, Basilica of St Mary in Cosme-
       din (1975), p. 27.
24   John 2:4 (New English Bible).
25   Mark 1:11 (New English Bible).
26   Amongst the works of the French cartoonist Jean-Paul Batelier.
27   Pablo Galdamez, op. cit., p. 8.
28   1 Corinthians 9:16.
29   Mark 4:1–8.

Creed

Echoes of the Truth

There comes a point, in each of the first three Gospels, where the whole mood changes. The first part of the story tells us who Jesus is, through the accounts of his birth, his baptism, his time of retreat in the wilderness, and then his 'public' ministry' of teaching and healing, seen chiefly through the gradually opening eyes of the disciples. Tradition limits the 'epiphany' of Christ to the stories of the Magi, the baptism, and the marriage at Cana: but really the whole of this first part of the gospel story is an epiphany, the 'showing' of the Son of God to his people. Most of the anecdotes in this section are set in the same area – Galilee – and quite a lot of the time we feel that their order isn't terribly important: what matters is the gradual but irresistible building up, in the minds of the original and the reading public, of the question 'who *is* this?', and of the answer which the evangelists want us to hear.

But then, in the second part of the story, everything changes: key, mood, tempo. Jesus 'sets his face towards Jerusalem',[1] from now on we are concerned less with who he is, more with what he is doing, where he is going: the forward shadow of the cross looms larger and larger, and it is the cross which lends meaning to everything that happens. From being a reasonably popular itinerant preacher, Jesus becomes the Suffering Servant, setting out on a hard and dangerous journey to the most ruthless of cities; the epiphany is over, the passion is ahead.

And the point of no return, the dividing line between these

61

two movements of the gospel story, is quite clear. It comes at Caesarea Philippi. The geography of the Gospels is easy to ignore, but, as here, is often tremendously significant: for Caesarea Philippi is at the very northern tip of the land of Israel, right beneath the slopes of Mount Hermon; the furthest away from Jerusalem that Jesus ever got. He leaves Galilee with his disciples in the opposite direction from Jerusalem, stops, and then, like a pendulum pulled right back for maximum effect, launches out on the final journey from which there is no going back.

Caesarea Philippi is the point of turning, the moment when the pendulum stops before swinging back. So the events around Caesarea Philippi represent the climax of the 'epiphany' stories, and the impetus for the 'passion' story, those few pregnant bars between one movement and the next. And what are those events? They are the final recognition, bursting out in Simon Peter's 'confession', of who Jesus actually is; and then, a week later, the 'showing' of Christ's glory on the Mount of Transfiguration.

And Jesus went out, and his disciples, into the villages of Caesarea Philippi; and on the road he asked his disciples, saying to them 'Who do people say I am?' They replied to him, saying 'John the Baptist; others Elijah; others one of the prophets.' And he asked them 'But you, who do you say I am?' In answer, Peter said to him 'You are the Christ.' . . .

And after six days Jesus took with him Peter and James and John, and led them up into a high mountain, all alone by themselves. And he was transformed in front of them, and his clothes became gleaming, exceedingly white . . . and there came a voice from the cloud: 'This is my Son, the beloved one: listen to him.'[2]

Such is the position of the Creed at the Eucharist. It comes at the still point between the two great movements of the Liturgy: the more static 'epiphany' section, the Ministry of the Word, confronting us with the person of Christ and his significance; and the more dynamic Ministry of the Eucharist, through which we enter once again into the self-offering, the death and resurrection of Christ. The still point is not a dead calm, but a moment of tension, an acclamation of faith in response to the Word, the Gospel and the sermon; and a drawing in of breath before we launch out upon our offering of Christ and ourselves.

But the Creed can easily become a point of deadness. For many people, if they are honest, it is a great stumbling-block, an ugly old monolith, interrupting the subtle flow of worship and replacing it with a bland ramming home of dogma; as if someone had come into a candle-lit room and switched on the strip lights. Everyone stands rigidly – sometimes, more militaristic still, all facing east – and signs on the dotted line of strict orthodoxy. Indeed, in the liturgies of the early Church, the Creed comes just at the point where the uninitiated have to leave, like a kind of gateway into the holy of holies: no one who doesn't believe all this can come any further.

But what is really going on? Do we really all believe every item of this fourth-century document? Is there, indeed, a congregation in the world where every single person believes with all their heart and mind every single item of the Nicene Creed as the literal, absolute and final truth of how things are and were? And what do we mean by 'believe', anyway? That we are prepared to accept these unlikely-sounding statements because the Church tells us to, shutting our eyes and trying hard; or that they are the most important truths of our lives? . . .

'How old are you?' [said the Queen].
'I'm seven and a half, exactly.'
'You needn't say "exactly",' the Queen remarked. 'I can believe it without that. Now I'll give *you* something to believe. I'm just one hundred and one, five months and a day.'
'I can't believe *that*!' said Alice.
'Can't you?' the Queen said in a pitying tone. 'Try again: draw a long breath and shut your eyes.'

Alice laughed. 'There's no use trying,' she said, 'one can't believe impossible things.'
'I dare say you haven't had much practice,' said the Queen. 'When I was your age, I always did it for half-an-hour a day. Why, sometimes I've believed as many as six impossible things before breakfast . . .'³

There is a great danger, if our belief becomes a matter of dogged will, that we will only be able to say the Creed when we have closed our minds to doubt and darkness and the voice which says 'it ain't necessarily so'. And there are strong pressures in today's Church to take such a line; but, if we are to enter into the true nature of the Creed and of Christian believing, it is important to see it, and to say it, in the context and the spirit of Caesarea Philippi.

And first of all this means recognizing that, however profoundly we may feel we have grasped the meaning of our faith, however well we may have articulated it, our particular profession of it is not, and never will be, the last word on the subject. Peter, of course, thinks it is, all the more so if Jesus has given him the pat on the back which Matthew records.⁴ But he shows in the next breath that he hasn't really understood the half of it: there is a whole lot more which can only become clear in the context of the way of the cross.

There is always a whole lot more. Faith, which stems from a relationship with the living God, can never be a closed book, any more than the body of Jesus could be kept shut up in the tomb. To claim to have the last word on divine truth, to have it all neatly sewn up, is a betrayal of the living faith which we profess. We may have made the most glorious discoveries, gained the most thrilling insights; they may be the truest things ever articulated by mankind; but, as soon as we make absolute claims for them, and begin to refuse to listen to the insights of others, they will turn to dust in our hands. We are, as the saying goes, *right in what we affirm but wrong in what we deny*.

This attitude, of denying that other people's different insights might have some validity, is what has classically been

known as 'heresy': the Greek word means 'choosing'; choosing
one truth at the expense of another, like the Six Blind Men
of Hindostan who all got hold of different parts of an elephant,
and argued respectively that it was like a wall, a spear, a
snake, a tree, a fan, and a rope:

> . . . And so these men of Hindostan
>   Disputed loud and long,
> Each in his own opinion
>   Exceeding stiff and strong,
> Though *each* was *partly* in the right
> *And all were in the wrong.*[5]

Within the early Church, similarly, one got hold of Christ's
divinity, another of his humanity; one of the distinction
between the three Persons of the Trinity, another of their
perfect unity; one of the necessary subjection of the Son to
the Father ('the Father is greater than I'), another of their
necessary equality ('I and the Father are one').[6] It was the
awkward and often costly task of orthodox theologians to
prevent the Church from slithering irrecoverably down one
side of either of these pairs of alternative, and apparently
conflicting, truths; and instead, stumblingly, painfully, to
work to *keep the gates open*, to make both sides of the truth
available, to insist on the essentially ambiguous and paradoxi-
cal (because living) nature of the faith. And it is in that
context that the Creeds were written, and it is in that spirit
that they should be said.

There is always more. The truth about God, the truth of God,
of his world, of his Kingdom, of his glory, can never be
exhausted: there is always more to be found, to be mined.
Jesus was the Word of God, but he didn't pretend to have
given the last word: as St John expresses it:

> Still many things I have to say to you,
> but you can't bear them yet;
> but when he comes, the Spirit of Truth,
> he will guide you to the truth in its fullness.[7]

The theology of the early Church was a part of this discovery of Christ's truth; there is much in the Creeds that goes beyond the insight of the New Testament. Of course: the Church had moved on, the setting, the age, the culture were all quite different. And now they are different again; we have moved on again; in our new setting the Spirit has still more to teach us.

If our faith is to be a living faith, we must be continually open to that teaching, never supposing we have the monopoly of the truth of God. And the teaching of the Spirit is given not through any direct flat plonking down of readymade truths from heaven, but in the sparking off of truth in encounter with what is strange, in dialogue with what is different, in the exploration of what others hold sacred. And this dialogue of the Spirit can lead us in so many directions.

It can lead us, first, to the encounter of our fellow-Christians. There are no two people in the world whose faith is identical; whenever two or three Christians meet and pool their deepest insights, the truth of Christ is revealed afresh: 'there I am' as he says 'in the midst of them'.[8] Groups for the sharing of our faith can be immensely fruitful, and all the more so (though the task is harder), when the encounter is with people of other denominations; when we dare for a while to drop our normal defence of assumed superiority and receive the riches of other traditions; when our own latent riches are so often teased out for the first time.

The dialogue of the Spirit is in the encounter of individuals and of different Christian traditions. Still, a further dimension is added when the encounter reaches also across the divisions of our world: when it is between people of a different social, racial, or educational background, or when it transcends national boundaries. We can learn so much from visits to or from Christians in other countries, and from those communities in the world which bring the nationalities together.

The dialogue can stretch across the world, and also down the ages. Perhaps the sharpest divide amongst Christians today is between the traditional and the modern; between those who look to the past for their insights and those who would sweep the past away. (Of course, this is not usually an absolute or clear-cut division: the most radical theologians are usually in the traditional churches, while those most impatient with 'tradition' are often extremely conservative in their theology.) Yet how vital these two strands are to each other: in church order as in theology, the new needs the old to ward off sectarian fanaticism, the old needs the new to save it from drying right up. The past and the present also need to meet: through the study of Christian history, and attention to the writings we have inherited.

But, finally (if anything can be final), we cannot confine the Spirit to the human boundaries of the Church or the Christian religion. If our faith is to live and grow, we must talk and listen to people from other fields and other faiths: to poets and philosophers, sociologists and politicians, mathematicians and astronomers, all who think and work at the frontiers of human knowledge and experience; to people of other religions than our own, those who come at God from a different angle, and those for whom God appears only as darkness.

But the encounter of Christians with other religions poses not only, sometimes, a threat, but also a difficulty: for, however much we may believe the Spirit breathes in the gaps and the tensions, how can any worthwhile truth spring from what is so often just a clash of opposites? Christianity affirms the fatherhood of God, Islam his absolute otherness; we say each human life is unique, many Eastern religions that the soul goes on from one life to the next; we claim one incarnation of God, the Hindus myriads, Jews and Muslims none at all. Surely the most we can hope from any dialogue here is to clear away a few misunderstandings and then to see our differences in all their starkness?

No doubt: but it is at this point that the encounter must move beyond a mere dialogue of words or ideas and into another world. There comes a moment where words begin to get in the way, and it becomes both possible and necessary to leave words behind. It is impossible to achieve any neat synthesis of ideas with Muslims or Hindus, but very possible, in silence, prayer, and sometimes also in action, to discover and celebrate a real community of the Spirit.

In the film *Sound Barrier*, the turning point came when the pilot discovered that, to fly successfully beyond the speed of sound, he had to reverse the controls of the aircraft: and so it turns out once we begin to break through the far more tremendous barrier of the knowledge of God. Up to a certain point, it made sense to say we are right in what we affirm and wrong in what we deny; but once we get at all near God, it is the other way round: affirmations become impossibly bland, inadequate, even blasphemous; God can only become known in the pillar of cloud, in the darkness, in the unknowing; only negative statements can make any sense. As we walk in faith through the wilderness towards the holy mountain, we have to abandon the words that seem to tie him down, relying only on the allusive and poetic; till finally even those must be left behind as faith and life and self all merge in the darkness.

Which brings us back to Caesarea Philippi. Here, too, Jesus leads his disciples from a spoken formula of belief into a mystical experience that strikes them dumb. When Peter makes his great affirmation: 'You are the Christ!', Jesus does not reply 'Yes, good, you have now grasped an eternal truth, necessary to salvation, which you must never question, and which you must ram home on everyone you meet, by fair means or foul', but something very different: *they are to tell no one about him*; the essence of his Christhood lies in the scandal of his coming death and resurrection; true belief involves travelling with him on this way of the cross.[9] Then, a week later, the experience of his transfiguration shows that belief is not finally a matter of saying the right formula, but of being caught up, body and soul, in the vision of glory.

All through his ministry, Jesus refuses to be labelled, categorized, tied down; labels cannot possibly express who he is or what he is about, and to bandy them around can only be damaging. At his baptism he is acclaimed from heaven as Son of God, but in the wilderness he utterly rejects the world's understanding of that title – privilege, glamour, power; and later on he always steers people away from such interpretations. He refuses to be proclaimed as a miracle-worker;[10] he rebukes the unclean spirits when they acclaim him as Messiah;[11] he even rejects the description 'good';[12] and in St John's account, where Jesus normally accepts titles much more readily, he 'withdraws into the mountains' when he realizes the people are about to come and make him king.[13] And now, again, when Peter acknowledges him as Christ, he responds with a tremendous protectiveness about the title – rightly as it turns out, for Peter has indeed misunderstood it. It is as if Peter has discovered something very precious but very very fragile, and Jesus is warning him not to drop it; as if, after a long vigil, he had finally spotted a rare and beautiful bird – talk in anything but whispers, and you'll frighten it away. And Peter, of course, does just that: he echoes the adulations of the devil in the wilderness, and Jesus rounds on him as on Satan himself.[14]

To be true to Jesus, then, we too must handle our belief delicately, we must speak our creed *pianissimo*. That is certainly the spirit of many of the early Fathers as they forged the first statements of Christian orthodoxy. Their theology was a 'feeble stuttering' in the face of the heretics, the 'choosers', who thought they had God's truth buttoned up. Augustine, writing on the Trinity, says this doctrine was formed '*non ut diceretur, sed ne taceretur*': not from any desire to speak, but from the impossibility of keeping silent.[15] Or, as St Hilary puts it,

> The errors of heretics and blasphemers force us to deal with unlawful matters, to scale perilous heights, to speak unutterable words, to trespass on forbidden ground. Faith ought in silence to fulfil the commandments, worshipping the Father, reverencing with him the Son, abounding in the Holy Spirit; but we must strain the poor resources of our language to express thoughts too great for words. The error of others compels us to err in daring to embody in human terms truths which ought to be hidden in the silent veneration of the heart.[16]

Words about God can never be more than a tentative and provisional representation of what must be utterly beyond words.

All our expressions of belief are partial and provisional. The third lesson of Caesarea Philippi is that faith only means anything if it is a commitment of the whole self, not just of the mind. This is such a strong theme of the New Testament that it hardly needs pointing out; but it's worth noticing that it appears at this moment also. It's the very next thing after Peter's confession: you can't have one without the other.

> And he began to teach them that the Son of Man must suffer many things, and be rejected by the elders and the chief priests and the scribes, and be killed, and rise again after three days; and he spoke this word openly . . .
>
> And calling together the crowd with his disciples, he said to them 'If anyone wants to come after me, let him deny himself and take up his cross and follow me.'[17]

Even at the transfiguration, according to Luke, suffering is part of the revelation: Moses and Elijah speak to Jesus of the 'exodus' he will accomplish in Jerusalem.[18]

In the same way our creed should be, not a list of satisfying propositions to roll off the tongue, but an act of commitment: *we are committed to* the creating power of God, *we are committed to* the saving work of Christ, *we are committed to* the new life of the Holy Spirit: all of which, if we take it seriously, will sooner or later mean a commitment to the cross. The creed of our words can only make sense within a creed of life. The words alone will mean more to some minds than to others, more indeed to me on some days than others – it depends so much on my mood, the weather, the pollen count, biorhythms, and the rest, whether every single phrase comes alive for me, or whether the whole thing seems dead and senseless – but what matters is not the momentary response of the mind, but the long-term response of life. The Creed is the gateway to the offering of Christ in the Eucharist; and, if it is forbidden to all but the initiated, that is not a test of orthodoxy, but because only those who are prepared *to be faithful* should be allowed to profess the faith: you can't believe in Christ without taking up the cross.

The reciting of the Creed will always – should always – be a slightly uneasy business. Few Christians could honestly say it is the best possible expression of what they do, in fact, believe; few, if asked to write down in their own words a list of their most cherished beliefs, would come up with anything much like it. But the Creed is not meant as a kind of minimal agreed statement – 'well, whatever else we think, at least we can all subscribe to *that*': rather it is a reminder and a challenge. It is a *reminder* that our personal believing, like the rest of our worship, is part of something far greater than ourselves; that what we personally can encompass with our minds and hearts may indeed be true, may even be a vital contribution to the whole body of Christian belief, but can never be more than a first step into the depths of the revealed and hidden truth of God. And it is a *challenge* to enter into dialogue and relationship with the believing of previous ages, and so to develop afresh a faith which is not merely the product of our own age and mentality, but which still addresses it in a way that can make sense.

In the early centuries, the first duty of a newly elected patriarch was to send round to his fellow-patriarchs the affirmation of his orthodox belief. So, as we rehearse the Creed together, we affirm our unity with every other member and part of the Catholic Church, and with our fellow-Christians down the ages and into the ages of ages. It is as if we were in an ancient cathedral with medieval paintings on the walls. Those paintings reflect a cosmology, and also, to some extent, a theology, quite foreign to us; if we had to paint the walls today we would never do them like that; yet we would never think of destroying or painting over them: we preserve them as a precious heritage, and, as we dwell with them and contemplate them, we begin to learn their language, to derive from them knowledge of God and great spiritual riches.

The Creed is not an unpleasant medicine for us to swallow, but a *gift* from the Church; something to enter into; a door into a large hallway, though not the only door or even the only hallway. It is not a prison cell, but territory to explore, to make our own, to become part of. Possible images are endless, but they all lead, in the end, to the presence of the living God who is beyond words and beyond images, who is not a list of concepts but a consuming fire.[19]

1   Luke 9:51.
2   Mark 8:27–29, 9:2–7 and parallels.
3   Lewis Carroll, *Through the Looking-Glass*, ch. 5.
4   Matthew 16:17–19.
5   'The Blind Men and the Elephant' by John Godfrey Saxe, in *The Book of a Thousand Poems* (Evans Brothers 1959), p. 484.
6   John 14:28, 10:30.
7   John 16:12–13.
8   Matthew 18:20.
9   Mark 8:30–31, 34–35.
10 See e.g. Mark 5:43.
11 E.g. Mark 1:25.
12 Mark 10:18.
13 John 6:15.
14 Mark 8:29–33.
15 Augustine, *de Trinitate*, tralatitious reference.
16 Hilary, *de Trinitate* 2:2, quoted by Maurice Wiles in *The Making of Christian Doctrine* (Cambridge 1967), pp. 32ff.
17 Mark 8:31–34.
18 Luke 9:30–31.
19 Hebrews 12:29.

6

Offering
The Whole World in His Hands

The first movement, the Ministry of the Word, is over: the epiphany has reached its climax on the Mount of Transfiguration; from now onwards Christ moves inexorably towards the cross. Beginning at the transfiguration, he prepares to offer himself in sacrifice, as he and his company approach Jerusalem.[1]

The priesthood of Christ was, is, radically different from the priesthood of the Old Covenant. Formerly – and still, in many religions – the priest offered to God, or to the gods, a substitutionary sacrifice, on behalf of the people; something other than himself, other than themselves, which would temporarily placate the heavens and take away from the people the burden of their sin. But this is not what Jesus did; he did not offer to God something alien, partial, or temporary: he offered up his whole self, and not just once upon a time, but always, for ever.[2]

The crucifixion sums up this self-offering, but it was not a once-off event. The whole life of Jesus was an act of self-giving; and not just from Caesarea Philippi, but from the beginning. The story is of a single selfless offering of obedience, from the obedience of Mary in Nazareth to the obedience of Jesus in Gethsemane, via so many other points of no return: birth, presentation, baptism, temptations, transfiguration, and the long hard road to Jerusalem. The cross was not an isolated propitiatory sacrifice, but the inevitable culmination of a life of love. The cross would make no sense apart from his life.

But, also, his life would make no sense apart from the cross. From the very beginning of the story, the cross casts its shadow backwards – in the Magi's gift of myrrh,[3] in Simeon's prophecy of the heart-piercing sword,[4] in Jesus' own predictions of his passion,[5] in the anointing at Bethany.[6] It was surely not because of any extraneous divine power that he could heal people and perceive their deepest needs; but because he was living a totally generous life leading – as all true love must – to the cross. As we contemplate his life, we can see that it takes its whole wonderfulness from being a life of self-giving, a life dedicated to the cross.

So the life and death of Jesus, his epiphany and his self-offering, are not in the end two independent things, the one to tell us the way to heaven by word and example, the other a priestly act which unlocked the gate for us. His priesthood permeates his whole life as it proceeds towards the mystery of the cross; and it is this complete act of self-offering, from conception to burial, which God vindicates at the resurrection.

As our High Priest, Christ did not offer something apart from himself, or only a part of himself: it was his whole life he offered. But even there it doesn't stop: for, as the Proper Man, he did not, does not offer to God only that one life 2,000 years ago; it was our human flesh he took, in our world, and it was our whole humanity and our world which, as our representative, he offered. The life of Christ – of humanity in the image of God – is not restricted to those few years on earth: his life, and thus also his offering, stretches from the dawn of creation into the ages of ages, and there is no limit to his embrace, as many fine hymns have put it:

> Out beyond the shining
> Of the furthest star
> Thou art ever stretching
> Infinitely far . . .[7]

and

> Crown him the Lord of years,
> The Potentate of Time,

Creator of the rolling spheres,
Ineffably sublime . . .[8]

In what sense is the Eucharist an offering? Protestant theology
has traditionally been very suspicious of language about the
'eucharistic sacrifice', insisting that Jesus made on the cross
(in the words of the Book of Common Prayer)

(by his one oblation of himself once offered)
a full, perfect, and sufficient
sacrifice, oblation and satisfaction
for the sins of the whole world.

Whereas we mere humans are

unworthy, through our manifold sins,
to offer unto thee any sacrifice . . .

or even

to gather up the crumbs under thy table.

Jesus made the only offering that was necessary, 2,000 years
ago; all we can do is to

continue a perpetual memory of that his precious death
until his coming again.

According to this theology we are purely on the receiving end
of what is being offered; there is nothing for us, in our total
unworthiness, to give, except for a rather indefinable 'sacrifice
of thanks and praise' – and of course our money.

With this theology we are firmly back in the dark world
described in Chapter 1: Jesus up there, the rest of us down
here; his sacrifice wholly different in scale and in kind from
any little offering we might make. But, if Jesus is not eternally
different in kind from the rest of us, but the first-fruits of
proper humanity, there cannot be an essential and eternal
divide between his offering and ours. He used and needed
our human flesh and blood as the material of his incarnation
and his sacrifice; so now he uses and needs our gifts of bread
and wine, and the lives and the longings they represent, as
the material for his self-giving at the Communion. And it is

our duty and our joy to unite our offering with his, at the Eucharist and in the world.

By writing Acts, Luke makes it clear that he sees the life of Christ continued in the life of the Church. His mission of teaching, healing and self-giving love is continued in the life and witness of the Apostles; his death in the deaths of Stephen, James and all the other martyrs. Paul makes the same point when he writes to the Colossians of 'making up in his flesh the incompleteness of the afflictions of Christ'.[9] And it is at the Eucharist that we most typically identify with the offering of Christ's life, summed up on the cross, and present it again and again to the Father; as the hymn puts it:

> One offering, single and complete,
> with lips and heart we say,
> but what he never can repeat
> he shows forth day by day.[10]

We do indeed 'plead the sacrifice of Christ' afresh at each celebration of the Eucharist – but not, as Catholic devotion has sometimes implied, to remind God of what Jesus has done for us, so that we could offer, even pay for, special Masses for special causes and so win extra favour with God, giving as it were a fresh jerk on the atonement lever; nor, on the other hand, as Protestantism often suggests, just to remind *ourselves* of what Christ did, and become once again the passive beneficiaries of his saving sacrifice. The Eucharist is not a pressing of the magic button in either of these directions – it is the means by which we are caught up in, and identify with, the sacrifice of Christ, joining our offering with his. The offering is *single*, but it will not be *complete* until he is able to offer to the Father the whole of humanity and the entire created order, when 'he delivers the Kingdom to God the Father after destroying every rule and every authority and power'.[11]

In the Eucharist we express our involvement in the sacrifice of Christ, an involvement which isn't restricted to an hour on a Sunday morning, but which flows out from there into the whole of our life, individual and corporate. 'Christ died for us'; yes, but not as a *substitute* for our dying and giving ourselves also, in our turn: rather in order that we may find the strength to die and give ourselves too – in order that we, as members of his Body, may live no longer for ourselves but for him, so that through us his arms may stretch wider and wider in their loving embrace of all creation and all of history. At the Offertory we bring to Christ the imperfect offering of our Christian life up to that moment; in the Consecration we unite our imperfect offering with his perfect one; and at the Communion, and afterwards, we are charged to continue his self-offering in the world.

The single offering of Jesus on the cross stretches out from Calvary across all time and space; in the Eucharist we identify with that offering, so that in us and in our gifts the pattern of his eternal incarnation, death and resurrection may be reproduced afresh. There is only one Eucharist; at every celebration we join in and add to it.

On the cross Jesus offered himself as the priestly representative of all humanity and creation. So, at the Eucharist, we, his priestly people, are not offering just Jesus, or just ourselves, or just these particular bits of bread and wine: we in turn stretch out our arms to embrace the world around us and to offer it along with ourselves. When the bread and wine are brought up to the altar, they represent not only our individual lives and concerns, not only the Church; but everything that has been going on around us, everything we have been involved in and everyone with whom we have been involved, whatever is on our minds and in our hearts and our prayers.

This is why the intercessions or bidding prayers traditionally come just before the offertory of bread and wine; they are, as it were, a formal expression of the world we are offering to God, the world of which we are the priest – both the external world and the world that is inside us. We offer our prayers, then we offer our bread and wine: the one flows into the other. It is as if the prayers were being brought up to the altar in the offertory procession along with the other gifts: a whole world, ready for consecration.

The offering of intercession is a vital link between the

Church and the world around; something is very wrong when the worship of a church is regularly without intercession. The people and happenings of the world *need* to be offered: one could even say that things only make sense if they *are* offered; and it is the job of the Church, as a priestly people, to make this offering. People without a formal Christian commitment often seem to recognize this; in their requests for prayers, in their delight when the Church shows an interest and their annoyance when it doesn't, in their need to talk which often feels like a need to be prayed for.

One powerful form of intercession is the 'litany': one person saying or singing a series of 'intentions', and everyone repeating a response. For public intercession is always a counterpoint between the 'official' prayers offered aloud (however informally), and the actual, heartfelt aspirations of the people. We need to be able to join our personal prayer to what is being said 'officially': so it can be helpful if some silence is included. Formal litanies are generally designed to encompass the widest possible range of human need; and the leader of less formal intercessions (whether prepared or extempore) also has the priestly task of expressing and offering what is in the air at the moment, of summing up the deepest concerns of the Church and the world. If she succeeds, then the response, whether it's an Anglican 'hear our prayer', an Orthodox '*Kyrie eleison*', or a Pentecostal 'oh *yes!*', will be heard to come from the heart.

The intercessor gathers up the prayers of the people and brings them to the altar, where, more often than not, the priest as it were puts the seal on them with a concluding sentence or collect. Exactly the same pattern is reproduced in the offertory procession: the sidesmen, or, in the original Orthodox tradition, the deacon, gathers up the gifts of the people and brings them to the altar where the priest offers them to God. So everyone takes part in the offering; and the exchange of the Kiss of Peace, which in the earliest tradition occurs at this point of the Liturgy, 'puts the seal on the prayers' as Tertullian said,[12] signifying that it is *one* offering, not from a collection of individuals, but from one people, united in Christ. In the words of St Cyril,

This kiss unites souls to one another and destroys all resentment. The kiss is a sign of the union of souls. This is why the Lord said: 'If you are offering your gift at the altar, and there remember that your brother has something against you, leave your gift there before the altar and go: first be reconciled to your brother . . .'

So, in the intercessions and at the Offertory, we unite to take the ordinary, half-created things and events of our world – as Christ took our ordinary, half-created humanity – and give them to God to bless and break and mould and give back, to use and to transfigure. And the ordinariness of what we are offering is a scandal, just like the parochial ordinariness of Jesus: 'Isn't this fellow the carpenter's son?'[13] . . . 'Can anything good come out of Nazareth?'[14]

This came home to me very forcibly when I said my second Mass. In the Catholic tradition, a priest's first Mass is the occasion for a rather self-indulgent but perhaps excusable jamboree: a great service, all one's friends and relations around, gorgeous vestments, special music, a visiting preacher; red roses for one's mother (or even wife), and a personal blessing for everyone present. My first Mass was like that, and it left me a good two feet off the ground with the wonder and joy and miraculousness of it all. But my second Mass! Two days later, round the corner in the side chapel, only two or three there, everything said and matter of fact and all over in twenty-five minutes . . . and I suddenly realized that I hadn't grown wings, the host wasn't dripping blood, indeed everything was quite ordinary and nothing overtly miraculous was happening at all.

Which, after all the build-up, was disconcerting; and it took me a good while to see that here, in fact, was the real spiritual experience: that God does not work through special effects, but through the ordinary and the everyday and the humdrum; his glory is 'hidden among the stuff',[15] as it was hidden in the bush by the wayside and in the life of the carpenter of Nazareth, and it is from there and there alone that it occasionally blazes out, as it did for Moses and for the three disciples up the mountain. For those things which we wrongly call 'ordinary' – including ourselves – are his creation, and so, at least potentially, very far from ordinary; and at the Eucharist he takes what is 'ordinary' and transfigures it: the bread and the wine and us and all our world . . .

> 'In a flash, at a trumpet crash,
> I am all at once what Christ is, since he is what I am and
> this Jack, joke, poor potsherd, patch, matchwood, immortal
>   diamond
> Is immortal diamond.'[16]

As in the incarnation, humanity and divinity are at last properly intermingled, and so the priest prays, as the water joins the wine:

> By the mystery of this water and wine
> may we come to share in the divinity of Christ
> who humbled himself to share in our humanity.

At the Eucharist, as in all sacraments, God uses our gifts, he consecrates the grubby and the ordinary: or perhaps, rather, since nothing is really 'ordinary', he takes what we have given and shows it to us as it truly is, free of the grime and greyness with which our sin and our blindness habitually cover it up. The giving at the Eucharist is not a one way thing, but, in the words of various offertory prayers, 'a holy exchange of gifts': we offer God what is 'ours', acknowledging that it is not truly ours but his – 'all things come from you, and of your own do we give you' – and he takes it and breathes into it the full glory of his life and power, and gives it back to us anew.

Our gifts are inadequate, certainly; but God understands that, for he knows our poverty and our weakness, and does not expect from us any angelic or superhuman perfection. It isn't perfection he requires of us, but *sincerity*: that we acknowledge the poverty of our offering, but give it with our whole heart, as 'the unleavened bread of sincerity and truth'.[17]

This theme occurs again and again in the stories of the New Testament. Jesus can accept and consecrate any offering, however pathetically inadequate, as long as it is given sincerely and without pretence. The widow's mite is worth more than all the rich men's fivers;[18] the sinful woman's tearful anointing is worth more than any fancy banquet;[19] and the hesitancy of the woman in the crowd,[20] the honestly uncertain faith of the epileptic boy's father,[21] carry more weight than the self-assurance of the inner circle of disciples. One small boy's packed lunch can feed a multitude;[22] water, poured out in faith, can become the very best wine.[23] Only what is given complacently or half-heartedly cannot be accepted: prayer that is pleased with itself,[24] people who are sure of their own righteousness.[25] Jesus longs to accept the 'lawyer' and the 'rich young ruler', but, before he can do so, he has to shake them out of their self-sufficiency.[26] And when the compassion of Jesus is no longer to hand, the theme is worked out much more harshly: witness the terrible story of Ananias and Sapphira in the Book of Acts.[27]

St John's account of the Feeding of the Five Thousand,[28] followed as it is by the great discourse on the Bread of Life, is clearly intended to refer us to the Eucharist. The disciples, like the deacons in the later, more developed liturgy, bring the gifts to Christ, who accepts them, blesses them, breaks them and shares them out. The ordinary becomes miraculous, the inadequate becomes abundant – so riotously abundant, in fact, that, like the wine at Cana, it can't be coped with. And now we are adding our loaf to the feast.

Another time a simple offering was made to Jesus was at Bethphage on the Mount of Olives, on the first Palm Sunday. A man lent his donkey; the people threw their garments on the beast and on the road, and strewed the way with greenery; and everyone shouted 'Hosanna!'[29] This offering also he accepted and blessed and transformed and shared, so that it became a royal procession into the Kingdom of God for us all to join in. And this, too, is paralleled, even relived, at the Eucharist, in the triumphant rehearsal of the great acts of God at the beginning of the Prayer of Thanksgiving, culminating in the very same acclamation:

Blessed is he who comes in the name of the Lord:
Hosanna in the highest!

81

But, just as the Palm Procession led to the Upper Room and to Calvary, so the triumph of the first part of the Prayer leads quickly to the Words of Institution and the Breaking of the Bread. Christ receives our offertory, our bread and wine, as he received our humanity; and he clothes himself in it; but in that clothing he is to be broken and poured out for the sake of the world; and in that clothing, warts and all, wounds and all, he is to be glorified.

So, in the Eucharistic Prayer, we offer afresh the sacrifice of Christ to the Father, and, as members of his Body, we become part of it. We have provided the instruments for the sacrifice, like Abraham with his fire and his wood:[30] here are the altar and the vessels and the 'elements', the bread and wine and water. But where is the lamb? The raw materials for the offering are lying around like Ezekiel's dry bones,[31] lifeless: the prophet has to prophesy to the Spirit for life to enter them, and so now we ask God to send his Spirit on these our gifts,

'that they may become for us
the Body and Blood of our Lord Jesus Christ,
at whose command we celebrate this Eucharist'.[32]

What is this 'consecration' we are praying for? It is, in fact, identical to *conversion*: we are asking for the conversion of our gifts *and of ourselves*. And the rather magical idea of consecration which some Catholics hold – that the priest says certain words and the bread and wine suddenly turn into something else – is very much paralleled by an equally magical idea (held by some Protestants) of personal conversion: that, from the moment someone 'becomes a Christian' (whatever precisely that may involve) he stops being himself and becomes someone else, an altogether different person. Rather obviously, none of this is true. The consecrated elements are obviously still bread and wine: the converted Christian is obviously still the same person. Of course, at first, he'll *feel* different: it is a wonderful thing to know Christ for the first time, to discover at last a new and meaningful direction for one's life. Life may indeed never be the same again: but the actual person, for better or for worse, remains very much the same. And it is harmful to pretend otherwise: 'now that I'm a Christian I never feel angry, or sad, or lustful, or jealous; now I'm a Christian I'm continually joyful; now I'm a Christian, in fact, *I am not as other people are*'. Apart from being insufferable to others, this attitude is damaging to one's self, because it really isn't true, and sooner or later it will mean keeping up an appalling pretence, to others and to one's self; sooner or later something will crack, and somewhere there will be a big mess to clear up.

Much of this stems from a misunderstanding, and sometimes a mistranslating, of St Paul. The Jerusalem Bible, for example, renders Romans 12:2 as

'let your behaviour change, modelled by your new mind'

which implies a sort of brain transplant at the moment of conversion, the slate wiped entirely clean; whereas the Greek says something like

'become reshaped by the renewing of your mind'–

a far more gradual process: we are discovering, uncovering, our true selves, becoming the people God has created us to be ... Again, the New International Version renders 2 Corinthians 5:17 as

'if anyone is in Christ, he is a new creation'

whereas the text, and its context, clearly say '*there* is a new creation'. What is brand new is not the person – as Paul knew only too well – but the situation, the direction in which the person is now facing, the light in which he is bathed. The 'new creation' is his relationship with God; it's the same old person, but alive with his love.

Very much the same applies to the conversion of the bread and wine at the Eucharist. Their constituent molecules are not suddenly reorganized into something different; but they – and we who are offering them – are as it were realigned, by identification with the person and the self-giving love of Christ; so that he can be experienced in them and through them, as he can (when we are true to him) in and through us his people.

This work of realigning, of putting people and things in the right setting, so that their true, and sacred, nature is revealed, is a work of *art*. There may be nothing obviously moving or beautiful or exciting about a particular word, or series of notes, or blob of paint, or piece of stone: but place it in the right setting, and both object and setting are transformed. This is what God, who is the ultimate artist, does in his consecration of us and our gifts; and it is also the artistic endeavour to which he calls us, his priestly people.

In many cultures there has been a strong linking, if not a complete identification, of the offices of poet and prophet, poet and priest. The poet is, or is like, a priest, overhearing the voice of God and relaying it as best he can; and the priest is, or is like, a poet (the word literally means 'maker'), placing the ordinary things of life in the setting of God, sacramentalizing them, showing up their true nature, causing a new created world to spring up. And, as with all art, the transformation often happens differently, more powerfully, than the poet herself could ever have imagined. Poets do not have the last word on the meaning of their own poetry; nor do priests ever fully understand their priesthood. But, in our Eucharist and beyond it, we continue to offer to God the puzzles and the glories, and the poverty, of our world and our lives, symbolized by these fragile gifts of bread and wine: and we continue to be astonished by what God makes of our offering.

The Eucharistic Prayer brings it all together: the offering of Christ, and of the Church – both the people there at the time and the great company of the faithful stretching across time and space – and the needs and wonders of the world, of all people living and departed. And, although thanksgiving may indeed be a part of what we have brought along, the true thanksgiving, Eucharist, is that which arises as God performs his artistic miracle, as the dry bones come to life, as the whole thing fits together, as the Holy Spirit does God's work of creation, making sense, transfiguration, resurrection.

Jesus, the great High Priest, has entered the holy of holies and stands before God in a perfect relationship of love; and now he takes us with him, and for a moment we too can stand beyond time, in the presence of the saints and angels and archangels, crying *Holy, Holy, Holy*. And, at the end of the prayer, we acclaim the offering with the 'great Amen' which St Jerome described as our 'thunderous applause'; then join even more closely with the offering of Christ, celebrating together his own prayer to the Father, the prayer he prayed in Galilee and in Gethsemane and on the cross, the prayer he prays now through his Church:

Your kingdom come,
Your will be done,
on earth as in heaven.

1 This is especially clear in Luke 9:51ff.
2 Cf. Hebrews 10:1–22.
3 Matthew 2:11.
4 Luke 3:35.
5 E.g. Mark 8:31, 9:31, 10:33–34.
6 Mark 14:8.
7 From 'Jesu, gentlest Saviour' by F. W. Faber, no 418 in *Hymns Ancient and Modern Revised*.
8 From 'Crown him with many crowns' by M. Bridges, no. 224 in *Hymns Ancient and Modern Revised*.
9 Colossians 1:24.
10 From 'Once, only once, and once for all', by W. Bright, no. 398 in *Hymns Ancient and Modern Revised*.
11 1 Corinthians 15:24.
12 *de Oratione* 19.
13 Matthew 13:55.
14 John 1:46.
15 1 Samuel 10:22, Authorised Version.
16 Gerard Manley Hopkins, 'That Nature is a Heraclitan Fire', and 'Of the Comfort of the Resurrection'.
17 1 Corinthians 5:8.
18 Mark 12:41–44.
19 Luke 7:44–47.

20   Mark 5:34.
21   Mark 9:17–24.
22   John 6:8–13.
23   John 2:5–10.
24   Luke 18:14.
25   E.g. Luke 14:7–11.
26   Mark 12:34, 10:21.
27   Acts 5:1–11.
28   John 6.
29   Mark 11:1–10.
30   Genesis 22:7–8.
31   Ezekiel 37:1–14.
32   From the 3rd Eucharistic Prayer of the Roman Missal.

7

Breaking
There Is No Answer

So far it has all flowed smoothly. We have come together as the Body of Christ, to celebrate, to align ourselves with, his offering: his incarnation, his life and his death. Whatever was amiss we have acknowledged at the Confession, looking forward in hope to the perfecting of our humanity in the image of Christ; we have experienced and responded to the Word and the Gospel; and all this, together with our prayers, we have drawn together and offered up in the bread and wine which represent for us the 'one, true, pure, immortal sacrifice' of Christ. The gifts have been consecrated, and will be given back to us at the Communion, the pledge of our own final consecration; so out we will go again into the world and the week ahead, refreshed and renewed for the service of God and of others. It all sounds good and satisfactory and worthwhile.

But now the bread is *broken*. Between consecration and Communion comes a messy discontinuity in the neat flow of the service, in the orderly scheme which seemed to be leading us so surely up to heaven. The beautiful host – or bun – is irredeemably broken and messed up: first by the hands of the priest, and then, as if that weren't enough, by the teeth, gullets, and guts of the entire congregation. At the very heart of what seemed so logical and well ordered, angelic almost, there breaks in, quite unexpectedly, this all too human act of disorder from which there is no going back.

So the Eucharist continues to represent accurately the sacrifice of Christ. How much neater if, as everyone expected of the Messiah, he had passed straight from a powerful life of teaching, healing and godly example, into the glory of heaven: as, indeed, docetists and Muslims and other groups believe that he did, as other saviours are supposed to have done. But the scandal of orthodox Christianity is precisely this terrible disorder, unneatness, brokenness, at its very heart: the incomprehensible, speechless awfulness of Good Friday – the failure, the tearing of the flesh, the agony, the death, the cross.

And the broken Body and the Blood poured out are also the scandal of the Eucharist. The early Church got a bad name for the 'cannibalistic' language of its rites, language which still arouses distaste in polite society today. Peter Shaeffer's Atahuallpah will always get a laugh when he says of the Christian God: 'First he becomes a biscuit, and then they eat him.'[1] It is such a strange unexpected climax to so much preparation and ceremonial, as strange and unexpected as the climax of the Messiah's life – the cross.

Yet, after all, it is the glory and the distinctive strength of Christianity that it has this brokenness at its heart; that, for all its wonderful systems and theologies and doctrines, our religion actually rests on a mystery, a scandal, a stumbling-block, a foolishness – on failure, silence and darkness. For that is, in fact and of course, what life is like: it *is* bloody and ghastly and brutish, and not all the dogmas and systems in the world can explain its bloodiness away. Salvation by neat answers is no real salvation, because it leaves the deepest questions to one side. There can be no 'answer' to Auschwitz or Aberfan or Hiroshima or Bhopal or Kampuchea, to mass starvation or multiple sclerosis, to Altzheimer's disease or AIDS; and any attempt to provide one – at least from outside the situation – can only be an affront, an obscenity; and, indeed, in the face of such uncomprehendable suffering and evil, all neat answers, even if they aren't addressing these particular questions, become a little trivial and absurd and irrelevant.

And that is how Christianity so often comes across. It is too neat. It is salvation by escaping from the bloodiness of life, by entering a clinical unreal world full of special words and nice people and wholesome unbloodiness. This can seem merely quaint, even rather delightful, as long as it merely involves leading a pleasantly sheltered churchy sort of life like some of the people in Barbara Pym's novels. It is only in the face of actual horrors – world poverty, or war, or individual suffering – that Christian escapism becomes downright sinister. If we remain determined to cling to our tight systems and neat answers in the face of *anything* that may happen, it must be at the expense of our humanity, our humaneness. Poverty? It is because they don't know Christ, who has promised prosperity to all his followers. War? But the other side are an evil empire, the agents of the Antichrist. Sickness? If you're a Christian, God will heal you; if he doesn't, it's a punishment for your sin. Job's three friends were trying to defend the system at all costs; and they are alive and well in the Church today.

Job, however, went on insisting that life *was* bloody and that there *were* no neat answers; and, when God answered him out of the whirlwind, his complaint was not that Job's words were blasphemous or doctrinally unsound, rather that he was daring to come at God with words at all. If there was a criticism of Job, it was that he was actually *too like* Eliphaz and Bildad and Zophar; he hadn't accepted their answers, but he had accepted their expectation of verbal answers.[2] Whereas God's 'answer' (which was not an answer) was storm and whirlwind and the singing of the stars and the extravagant wild riches of creation and the impossible hilarious monsters of the deep:[3] evoking not words but silence and awe and darkness and brokenness and faith.[4]

And the darkness and brokenness of the cross are in the end the only authentic 'answer' Christianity can provide to the darkness and brokenness of the world. Of course there must be provisional answers; of course there are times when faith is stretched to breaking-point, and the question 'why?' cannot be avoided; and the priest and the pastor and the theologian and the congregation can't just ignore the question and go on wallowing in a wordless mire of mystery, they must come to grips with it as best they can. Words are necessary and often helpful: as long as we remember that they aren't, and cannot be, the last word. For if there were a 'last word' on the problems of suffering and evil, they would long ago have ceased to be problems, and gone back into the file with a nice tick against them – 'Job done!' – like the problems of why the moon has eclipses, or how you tell the time in mid-Atlantic, or how you eradicate smallpox from the earth, and so many others which need no longer concern us.

We have no last word, no neat explanation, of the mystery and bloodiness of life: we have only the cross. Christ does not say: Don't worry about your suffering, it will all be all right in the end, it's all (did you but know it) meaningful and necessary and good. He says only: Here I am on the cross also, forsaken by God but refusing to come down. And that must be our answer too, again and again . . . as Daniel Berrigan has put it,

> There is no answer.
> The genius of the gospel is in the name of man
> to refuse an answer[5]

and also, we could add, in the name of God: I have no answer, I share your bewilderment, I appreciate your bitterness, and, though I can never even properly understand how you feel, here I am for what it's worth, in it with you, inadequately holding your hand and at least refusing to escape, either physically into my own lack of suffering, or mentally into my neat solutions and dogmas.

The cross is at the heart of our faith, and brokenness and messiness at the heart of our Eucharist. Jesus didn't jump from Maundy Thursday to Easter Sunday, and we don't jump neatly from consecration to new life. The bread and wine of our offering represent a broken world: Christ took upon himself the sin of that world, and we in our turn have offered badness and poverty, doubt, tears, sickness, disunity and unwholeness at every level. Unbroken bread would not truly express our world or our offering; the breaking of bread and the pouring out of wine reflect more accurately its brokenness and its bloodiness.

But more than this: our role here is not neutral, we are not just recalling the death of Christ and the brokenness of the world for the sake of general edification. Like him, we are no 'hired man whose own the sheep are not',[6] no 'high priest who is unable to sympathize with our weaknesses';[7] we are offering not only Jesus, not only bread and wine, not only the world, but ourselves also in this sacrifice. Far from being an escape from the world's darkness and pain, our Christianity is calling us to offer ourselves in sacrifice for that darkness and pain. When we cry 'Lamb of God, have mercy on us', it doesn't mean 'for God's sake get us out of here!', it means 'Lord, we're in here, at the heart of the world's sin and pain, as you were: help us to bear it as you did.' To enter the darkness and the discontinuity is our only means of salvation.

Salvation through the cross – easy to say, hard to comprehend. The temptation is to make it mean 'Christ died on the cross for me, so I can escape the cross; salvation is easy, the way to heaven is easy, because Jesus has got me there; he's done it all, so I don't need to do anything.' Such is not the witness of the New Testament. Christ has not taken our cross away: he tells us we must shoulder it. But he *has* transformed it: 'The tree of shame was made the tree of glory, and, where life was lost, there life has been restored.'[8] Being saved by the cross does not mean escaping the cross, but embracing it. And furthermore that is *all* it means – we embrace the cross with no ulterior motive,

'not for the sake of winning heaven
or of escaping hell . . .'[9]

The nature of our salvation is well illustrated by the story of James and John coming to Jesus and asking for reserved seats in the Kingdom, one at his right hand and the other at his left. Jesus, in reply, asks if they are able to drink his cup and share his baptism – both symbols of his obedient acceptance of suffering and death. Yes, they say, we are able. Very well, says Jesus, you will share my cup, you shall undergo my baptism; but as for seats on my right and on my left, sorry, I can't promise anything.[10]

At first reading it sounds as if Jesus has pulled a fast one on his two disciples. In their eagerness for the seats of honour they accept his cup and his baptism; but, once these have been accepted, the original prize is withdrawn. But, in fact, Jesus is showing them the only way to the Kingdom, and it *is* a narrow way: it is the way of renouncing *all* self-interest, even the desire to save one's soul. 'For whoever wishes to save his soul will lose it; but whoever loses his soul for my sake and for the gospel's, shall save it.'[11]

We are not called to live lives of sacrificial love because that will get us to heaven; love with an ulterior motive is hardly love. We are called to such living and loving for its own sake, ignoring the rewards and punishments, just walking, with Jesus, from moment to moment on the way of the cross. It is unthinkable that, all through his long journey to Calvary, Jesus was actually saying to himself, 'Well, it'll be hard for a few hours, but it'll be worth it, because after three days I shall rise again and after forty-three I shall be back in heaven', as I used to comfort myself with the thought of buttered toast during obnoxious games of rugby at school. The evangelists knew what lay ahead as they wrote, but surely Jesus didn't, otherwise all his agony and forsakenness must seem quite contrived. The cross was a *real* discontinuity, and he embraced it, not because he knew it led somewhere else, but because it was the only possible way forward if he was to be true to himself and his mission and his vocation.

To lose his life was the only way to save it. Had he come down from the cross, he would have saved his life but been untrue to his deepest self; in other words, he would have lost his soul: as it was, he lost his life but saved his soul. But the cross wasn't a step, even *the* step, towards salvation, a necessary hiccup on the way to resurrection: the cross was salvation. The laying down of life was not a stage on the way to the Kingdom: it was the Kingdom itself. In Luke's account, Jesus promises salvation to the repentant thief not in two days' time but *today*;[12] while, in John's Gospel, it is the cross, not something beyond the cross, which is spoken of as the hour of Christ's glory.[13]

When Jesus offers his cup and his baptism to James and John, he is not dodging the issue of the Kingdom, he is actually revealing it. To forget all about salvation is to achieve salvation; to share his cup and his baptism *is* to sit beside him in the Kingdom, though one might not notice one was doing so. So, in the same chapter 10 of Mark's Gospel, as Jesus makes his way down the Jordan valley towards Jerusalem, he commends the uncomplicated approach of children to the Kingdom, tells the rich young man to forget worldly interests and take up his cross, and foretells his own coming death. And so with us now: at our baptism we renounced all self-interest, material and spiritual; and we renew our commitment to the cross at every Eucharist, each time we break Christ's Bread and share his Cup, 'proclaiming the Lord's death until he comes'.[14]

At this breaking of bread we offer all the brokenness of our lives and of our world, not neatly, or in the certainty of answers, but as Christ did, in faith and in silence of heart. And we offer also whatever still needs to be broken: our riches, our false adulthood, our desire for glory; and, like James and John, we accept the cup of Christ as the only thing of ultimate importance. We can only be ourselves as we are poured out in love for God and for others, such is our salvation.

Catholic tradition stresses the value of reverence for the consecrated bread and wine, particularly by the custom of genuflecting, bending the knee as we approach the altar, or the tabernacle where they are reserved. But what are we reverencing? Not cold, static objects made holy by valid formulae; but the bread in its brokenness, the wine poured out, the life of Christ given for us. In bending the knee we offer our whole body, we lay down our whole life, before this sacrament of unstinted love, assenting, responding, attuning our whole self to the self-giving of Christ. We are not adoring from a distance, but making a physical sign of our own sacrifice, united with the sacrifice of Christ.

And so with the Lord's Prayer: here again, as we pray for the hallowing of the Father's name, the coming of his Kingdom, and the doing of his will, we are not asking that these things should happen apart from us, just because Jesus asked it long ago. He gave us his prayer to be our prayer, and, repeating it, we offer ourselves in our turn as the instruments of his glory, his kingship, and his will; praying with all our hearts that earth may become like heaven, that earth and heaven may be one, that what we anticipate at this feast may one day be reality; and asking for the courage to eat, with him, the Bread of the Kingdom.

Meanwhile the discontinuity remains. Earth is not yet heaven, and our attempt to anticipate heaven on earth can only go so far, issuing finally in brokenness, silence and darkness. A perfect world would have acclaimed a perfect priesthood, embracing the perfect communion that was offered. But Jesus' priesthood was not acclaimed, was indeed violently rejected; people would *not* join his dance, he was not able to carry the world with him. Instead he had to be set against the world, and to be offered up, not alongside the people but in their stead, a scapegoat who carried their sins.

And such has always been the calling of his Church: to try to work with and for his world, but to end up over against it, rejected, persecuted, thrown out and killed – yet still pleading on the world's behalf. The prophets were stoned, slaughtered and ignored; the witnesses of the Christian Church were rejected and put to death ... and still it goes on, in the clear shining martyrdoms of Luther King, Jerzy Popieluszko, Janani Luwum or Oscar Romero, and in the more obscure martyrdoms of countless Christians misunderstood and rejected at home, at work, in the world. What makes a 'successful' Christian, a successful church? So often we give the palm to the church with everything going for it, with big congregations and swelling numbers, wealth and strength and activity, firm belief, sound behaviour, gifts of the Spirit past counting; and to the individual who shines with faith or wholeness or authenticity. These can indeed be a cause for rejoicing; yet I wonder if in the Kingdom of Heaven it is not sometimes the poor little Christians who will come first, the failures, the broken ones, the sort of people who are heroes in Graham Greene novels, or like Peter Sellers' vicar in *Heavens Above!*, rejected by the world and finally made Bishop of Outer Space.

The bread is broken, the wine poured out, the invitation

given. The banquet is ready, and who will come? Again there is good news and there is bad news. The bad news is that we can't come in unless we bring our whole selves; there is no part of us, like our riches or our pride, which can be left intact and taken up again just the same when we leave; we must have on the wedding garment of sincerity. Like Jesus, we must lay down our whole life. But the good news is that, if we do indeed offer our whole selves, they will never be rejected or turned away, however grubby or inadequate they may seem. Those who appeared to deserve a place at the wedding feast gave only a halfhearted response and were turned away: the rest, quite inappropriate people really, responded gladly and were made welcome.[15] None of us, in the end, is worthy to come under the Lord's roof or to have him under ours; but he speaks the word for us and it's good enough.[16]

Someone once asked Brother Roger of Taizé to tell the assembled young people that God was not asking too much of them. His reply was simple: '*Il ne demande pas trop – mais il demande tout*', he doesn't ask too much – but he asks everything.

1 Peter Shaeffer, *The Royal Hunt of the Sun* (Samuel French 1964), Act II, scene 4 (pp. 37–8).
2 Job 38:1–2, 40:1–2.
3 Job 38—41.
4 Job 42:1–6.
5 Daniel Berrigan, §11, ll. 1–4 of his Foreword to *Quotations from Chairman Jesus*, compiled by David Kirk, Templegate Publishers, Illinois 1969: quoted by John Taylor in *The Go-Between God* (SCM Press 1972), p. 146.
6 John 10:12.
7 Hebrews 4:15.
8 Alternative Service Book, Holy Communion Rite A, preface 10 (p. 155).
9 From 'O Deus Amo Te', translated by E. Caswall, no. 106 in *Hymns Ancient and Modern Revised*.
10 Mark 10:35–40.
11 Mark 8:35.

12 Luke 23:43.
13 E.g. 12:23, 17:1 (cf. 3:14–15).
14 1 Corinthians 11:26.
15 Matthew 22:1–14.
16 Matthew 8:5–13.

8

Communion
Yes to Life

The Eucharist is our Christian sacrifice: an uncomfortable truth, all too often forgotten or avoided. Not just a framework for God's gift, not just a glorified and stylized meal; but an offering, in fact *the* offering, ours united with Christ's. We are caught up in the self-giving of his life and his death. As he took flesh then in a human body, so he takes it now in the bread and the wine and the lives which we offer: as he gave himself up then on Calvary, so now at our altar the bread and wine are broken and shared; everything we have is put at God's disposal. In this utter self-giving the Kingdom and the will of God are made known, and we kneel and adore.

Wonderful, but sombre: as sombre as if the cross, for all it is a sign of love, were the last word on the Christian Gospel; as if Holy Week ended on Good Friday. And so much of our liturgy has made it seem so. The Tridentine Mass and the 1662 Communion Service, much as they differ in other ways, have in common a distinct absence of the Easter spirit: both concentrate heavily on death and sacrifice and bounden duties. The very words of Communion in the Prayer Book service hammer home the death of Christ:

> The Body of our Lord Jesus Christ, which was given for thee, preserve thy body and soul unto everlasting life.
>
> Take and eat this in remembrance that Christ died for thee, and feed on him in thy heart, by faith with thanksgiving . . .

Drink this in remembrance that Christ's blood was shed for thee, and be thankful.

Awesome, certainly, but hardly steeped in the joy of the resurrection. Yet, in the gospel narrative as in the liturgy of the Church, Good Friday is not the end of the story. Jesus gave himself up, in his life and on the cross, finally and totally and irreversibly; he suffered death and was buried: but God vindicated him by raising him from the dead, and it is his *risen* Body which we celebrate and receive in the Holy Communion.

God raised Jesus from the dead; but the resurrection of his body was and is, by all accounts, something very different indeed from a mere continuation of his bodily life, as if the two days among the dead were just a hiccup in the story of the physical Jesus. The French have got it extremely wrong in speaking of *le Christ ressuscité*, as if he had merely come back to life again, as if the resurrection of Christ were in the same class as the raising of Jairus' daughter. This is the start of something completely different, a wholly new form of life and being: 'Even if we used to know Christ according to the flesh,' says St Paul, 'yet now we no longer know him [so]'.[1]

That was certainly the experience of the disciples in the gospel story. It is strange that, in the resurrection narratives, they again and again fail to recognize the risen Christ: in the garden,[2] on the road to Emmaus,[3] in the Upper Room,[4] by the lakeside.[5] Although at first he does have some sort of appearance, it clearly isn't physical in the ordinary sense: he appears and disappears, he gets through locked doors, he can't be held down. And in the fourth Gospel, where in a sense we are dealing throughout with the risen Christ, he is presented not just in human and physical terms, but as transcending ordinary physical laws – changing water to wine, walking on the sea, multiplying the loaves, raising the dead – and in a whole series of powerful and bewildering images: as bread, wine, light, truth, life. I AM! he declares again and again, echoing God's word to Moses: he is eternally present, not constrained by time and space.

This is well expressed by Sydney Carter in his song 'The Lord of the Dance':

I danced on a Friday when the sky turned black;
it's hard to dance with the devil on your back.
They buried my body and they thought I'd gone . . .

Now if Jesus had merely 'come back to life', he could have finished the verse:

but I hadn't really died, so I came back on;

or:

but I'm actually alive, I go on and on and on . . .;

instead, he sings of the true resurrection by adding a new I AM saying to John's list:

but I AM the dance, and I still go on.

During his earthly life, he was leader of the dance; now he actually *is* the dance.

Another effective portrayal of the resurrection is in the musical *Godspell*. When this first appeared on the London stage, a group of severe Christians stood outside to protest, because, they said, it didn't include the resurrection: in other words, the physical Jesus didn't come back on. But reappearances on stage of the physical Jesus – looking much the same as he did before – are always a dramatic anti-climax, as well as suggesting a merely resuscitated Christ. *Godspell* gets far closer to the truth. Jesus dies. There is silence. Then the disciples very slowly begin to carry his body off the stage, and very slowly begin the singing of 'Long live God'; echoing, at first, the sad triumph of Good Friday. But then a new note creeps in: the song gets faster, and above the refrain 'Long live God' reappears the original song of John the Baptist: 'Prepare ye the way of the Lord.' The cast begins to dance and the audience begins to clap; as at Pentecost, the story is starting afresh, within the body of believers. The true resurrection is not just one more in a long line of remarkable events; it is a new kind of thing altogether, a meta-event, the conversion of death into life and of life into glory.

This same spirit of wordless wonder breathes through the extraordinary drama of the Church's own Easter Liturgy. In the most Protestant of churches there is something exciting in the Easter air, if only extra flowers and a fuller church: in the Catholic tradition, this above all is a liturgy which goes beyond words, with its rich use of symbol and suggestion: darkness and silent anticipation; new fire, and the gradually spreading light of the paschal candle; the explosion of sound at the *Gloria*; the delight and relief of the first *Alleluia* since Lent began. As with all ritual (including the ritual of words) there is a danger that these might become empty symbols; but it is hard not to glimpse somewhere amongst them at least the shadow of the risen Christ, not browbeating us with solid evidence, but going tantalizingly on ahead, into Galilee and goodness knows where.

And, although it is only officially Easter once a year, every Sunday is the Day of Resurrection, a little Easter; and every day is a little Sunday. There is always something of Easter in the liturgy, even on Good Friday; and the very decoration of churches always speaks, or at least whispers, of the risen Christ. Above all he has transformed the *altar*, which represents for us the cross of Christ . . .

An altar stands within the shrine,
whereon, once sacrificed,
is set, immaculate, divine,
the Lamb of God, the Christ . . .[6]

but our Cross is not merely an old rugged cross on a green hill far away without a city wall, it is something gleaming with life; as the Dreamer saw it,

. . . adorned with streamers, shining with things of joy,
garnished with gold; gems had
worthily wrapped the tree of the Almighty.
But through that gold I could well perceive
how the wretched had striven, so it soonest began
to sweat on the right side. I was all disturbed with sorrows,
fearful at that fair sight. I saw that beacon in its haste

100

changing dress and colours: now it was drenched with
   wetness,
soaked with the stream of blood; now adorned with
   treasure.[7]

So our Christian altar is not just a grim slab of stone prepared
for sacrifice, it has become the table of the feast of life, decked
with fair linen and candles and ever-changing colours. Instead
of finding ourselves at Mount Sinai with its

burning fire and stormy darkness and gloom and tempest
   and the trumpet's echo and a voice of utterances
whose hearers begged that not a word should be added
   to them,
for they could not bear the special command, that
'if even a wild beast touches the mountain, it shall be
   stoned':[8]

here we are rather at the heavenly Jerusalem, welcomed by
an innumerable company of saints and angels. The chalice,
the sign of the ultimate sacrifice, has been transformed into
the sign of God's ultimate graciousness, beckoning us to the
feast. And the great and terrible I AM, who blazed out at his
servants from the bush and the mountain, is now made known
through symbols of familiar welcome, as bread and light and
vine and shepherd. Far from terror now, we can 'go in and
out and find pasturage'.[9]

From now on the life of Jesus can't be contained, in a human
body or any other sort of tomb: churches or laws or systems
or dogmas. He can't be held down or boxed in, by foes or by
friends. If ever we think we've got him taped, he eludes us;
whenever we think we've lost him, there he is . . .

I try to flee, but he says follow,
I try to go, but he says stay,
I shut my eyes, but still he beckons,
I try to run – he bars the way.

Catch the echo of his footsteps,
Catch the rustle of his cloak:

Was that his shadow in the sunshine?
Was that him who spoke?

Catch him if you can, catch the Living Water,
Catch him if you can, try to catch the world's True Light.
Follow, follow if you dare, down the winds of Heaven,
And you shall find in him your heart's delight.[10]

'If the seed of the grain does not fall into the ground and die', says Jesus to Andrew and Philip in John 12:24, 'it remains itself, alone: but if it dies it bears much fruit.' So the Body of Jesus was sown in the earth, and died, and rose up again, no longer a single physical body, able to be confined; but a spiritual body which all the disciples and priests and Romans, and tyrants and sceptics, and preachers and theologians and bishops and inquisitors in the world have been unable to hold down ever since. He won't stay in the safe and respectable places; more likely he'll be found, as in his earthly life, amongst the poor and the unrespectable, the tearaways and the dropouts and the failures, the non-Christians and the unbelievers; more likely in pubs than in vestries, in reggae and wild poetry than in hymns and tracts; in dances and parties than in services and synods; leading not a religious procession but a bacchanalian conga which turns everything in its path inside out and upside down.

It was no good clinging to the physical Jesus after his resurrection. 'Don't cling on to me,' he says to Mary in the garden.[11] 'Why stare up into heaven?', the two angels ask the disciples.[12] He has gone; let him go. 'Unless I go away,' he says in John 16, 'the Spirit will not come to you.' So the disciples, and the early Church, bid farewell to the bodily Jesus, and greet him anew as the living presence in their midst. The Epistles hardly ever refer to his earthly life, and even the Gospels – the fourth especially, but the others also – are, though based upon his life, far more concerned with the present, living Christ than with the chronicling and recapturing of the past. The Church doesn't relate to Jesus as a past historical figure or as someone up in the sky with God; but in a new and radical way, as the living head, cornerstone, heart of its present life; as its very character and personality, in whose name it preaches and prays and heals and baptizes; and, at Emmaus and ever since, in the breaking of the bread. From the resurrection onwards, Jesus is known not by his face but by his glorious *wounds*, and by this eucharistic action which enables us to identify with them.[13]

More recently, the Church hasn't been so good at letting go of Jesus. We speak of him as being 'alive' as though he were somehow still around, though no one ever actually sees him. I once heard a sermon which quoted with approval a convert who said he no longer felt happy sinning, because now he knew Jesus was always looking (Big Brother-like) over his shoulder. But, even if we don't consider him as 'around' in this spectral sense, we are still inclined to put up spiritual ladders and towers to reach him in heaven; focusing all our energy and attention on a distant figure who may perhaps one day come again, rather than on our vocation, now, to be his Body in the world.

We don't take seriously enough the radical, intolerable statement of St Paul that, here and now, *we* are the Body of Christ.[14] Jesus isn't alive somewhere else, but here, in our midst:

> The kingdom of God doesn't come with observation,
> and they won't say 'Look here!' or 'there!';
> for look, the kingdom of God is in your midst.[15]

We discover the risen Christ wherever the pattern of his saving wounds is reproduced; wherever there is self-giving love, wherever suffering becomes redemptive, wherever the cross is *taken up* rather than merely endured. And sometimes this happens within the Church and sometimes it doesn't: but, just as Jesus broke bread and poured out wine as the sign of his coming sacrifice, just as he was thereafter recognized in the breaking of the bread; so we repeat the eucharistic action as the pledge, the earnest, of our identification with his sacrifice, our willingness to reproduce his wounds, our vocation to be his Body.

And so, when we receive the broken bread and the wine at the Communion, we are asked to affirm our participation in the Body of Christ, our willingness to be poured out for his sake, with a strong personal Amen – *Yes!* Some traditions use a longer form of words when the Communion is shared (like 'The Body of Christ keep you in eternal life – Amen'); but these longer forms are also weaker, because they narrow down what is being said to a mere prayer for individual salvation. The short form is stronger, more all-encompassing. 'The Body of Christ – Amen; the Blood of Christ – Amen.' This is indeed a personal affirmation, a joyful welcome of the risen Saviour, like Mary Magdalene's: Oh, yes, Lord, it is you, you are here in our midst and in my life . . . and we are told in Revelation that Amen is actually one of his names:

Thus says the Amen, the witness, the faithful and true, the beginning of God's creation . . .[16]

As I receive the Sacrament, I am greeting Jesus with a nickname: the transaction isn't just for my benefit, to 'keep me in eternal life', but something worthwhile in itself, a lovers' meeting, a moment of truth. Christ comes to me as before, weak, poor, vulnerable, and beautiful, full of life; he accepts me completely, giving himself for me, welcoming me into the Kingdom of his Body; and I answer Amen, acclaiming him as the final truth of my life.

In this important sense I am indeed 'making my Communion' when I say Amen to the bread and wine: it is a moment of profound personal Communion with the risen Christ. He welcomes me as someone utterly precious: but he welcomes me not to an otherworldly *tête-à-tête* but to participation in his Body in this world; and to this too I assent with my Amen. Yes, I have died to my selfish self in baptism, and my life now makes no sense apart from Christ's Body; yes, as a member of that Body I am now willing, in his name, to be broken and poured out for his people and his world. The Real Presence, from now on, is us.

And 'us' in the broadest possible sense. In the Communion as at the Peace, I am saying Yes to those around me at the altar: but my Yes goes beyond the church I can see: it is also a Yes to the Apostolic Church from the Day of Pentecost onwards, to my communion with all the holy women and

men there have ever been and ever will be; it is a Yes to the
catholic Church across the world, to my fellow-Christians in
every continent; to those from whom I am divided by human
narrowness and sin, whether they are (to use the blasphemous
language of the world), in 'other communions' or in 'enemy'
lands; to those who are poor, and to those who are even now
making a costly witness to the faith of Christ and the truth
of God.

All this is the Body of Christ to which I say Amen; but my
Yes goes further still, from real to imaginary numbers, from
the actual Church to the potential. I am affirming, too, all
those people of God who know him by another name and
worship him in other ways; all those 'holy and humble of
heart' who cannot use the name of God, often for profoundly
spiritual reasons; and, in the end, that spark of true humanity,
true divinity, which waits, however dormant, in every single
human soul, however apparently sinful and beyond the pale,
and whether still alive, beyond the grave, or yet to be born.
And I say Yes to my brothers and sisters the animals, the
plants, the sea and the stones, the planets and the stars, the
powers, the angels, and the whole of creation whose song I
can sometimes, in moments of longing, just faintly catch, but
in which one day, when Christ is all in all, I shall fully join.

For this meal, this Communion, is an anticipation, a foretaste
of the heavenly banquet. Of course the Communion which
we celebrate is not yet realized; of course I could not be
thinking about so many levels of peace and unity during my
brief visit to the altar rail, and, even if I could, I would have
to admit that most of them are far from present fulfilment,
either in the reality of the external world or in the 'dust and
sinne'[17] of my own soul. The world is not at peace; the Church
is not one Body; I do not feel total love for everyone around
me, even for the other people in church; most likely I am not
at all at peace within myself. Should I therefore say this
Amen? Should I take Communion at all?

Maybe there are times when the right answer is No. Rowan
Williams commends Henry II for refusing the Peace to
Thomas Becket;[18] and, in his moving description of a Masai

village Eucharist, Vincent Donovan speaks of the times when
he was told that there could be no Eucharist because the
village was not 'at peace'.[19] We should take note of this, not
slip into a too easy Communion which glides meaninglessly
over our unhealed emotions and relationships.

But, in this guilt-ridden world, the danger is much greater
of being too harsh on ourselves, of persisting in our sense of
unworthiness when God, after all, has made us worthy: 'If
God has justified, who is to condemn?'[20] There is much talk
of 'hypocrisy' within the Church, and this often spills over
into an idea that we may be being 'hypocritical' in daring to
come to Communion. But very few people really exchange
the Peace or receive Communion with pure cynicism, and
there are more miracles of healing and reconciliation within
the humdrum old church than is often acknowledged; for
the Sacrament is both our pledge, and God's means, of
at-one-ment.

Things may not be right between me and Mary, but I can
use the Kiss of Peace to put them right – or at least as a
beginning, as a sign of my ultimate desire that they should
be right. Things may not be right between me and God; but
all of Jesus' teaching and the Church's tradition make it quite
clear that we can never get into the banquet on the strength
of our worthiness, only at his gracious bidding. As in George
Herbert's poem, our souls draw back, but he insists:

'You must sit down,' said Love, 'and taste my meat':
So I did sit and eat.[17]

The Communion, like the resurrection, anticipates the Kingdom of Peace: it is the start of a putting right, inside me,
within the Church, and so, ultimately, for the whole world.
The Sacrament is not just a symbol of what might be one
day: it is an effective sign, the sowing of the seed of the
Kingdom. It may bring home to us how far we are from the
true Communion of that Kingdom, but its message is one not
of guilt and despair, but of hope: the seeds of Communion in
your life will flower, a sign of grace for the whole world.

The same arguments apply to questions of 'intercommunion' between the different and unreconciled branches of

the Church. Is intercommunion a too easy glossing over of our differences, a papering over of the cracks, or is it the expression of a fundamental unity more real than all our human divisions? Once again, there is something to be said for not carrying on as if there *were* no divisions, for facing the sin that is there. It is painful, as an Anglican priest, to attend a Roman Catholic Mass in an official capacity and be unable to receive Communion; it is painful to attend a concelebrated Mass and be debarred from participating. But, it can be argued, this pain is only the surface expression of a real illness, and so, like all healthy pain, is a good thing – we should not be trying to heal the superficial pain, but go to work on the underlying disease.

There is something in this: such pain can certainly be a spur to ecumenism, while, conversely, easy intercommunion among the Protestant churches has often led to premature complacency: 'We get on well enough, we have intercommunion, what more need we do?' But in the end the argument is unacceptable. The Eucharist, and the Holy Communion which it enshrines, is not meant to be an expression of how the Church is on earth, now; but of how it is to be, finally, in God's Kingdom. And the very first attribute of the true Church, which we affirm in the Creed, is that it is – it is to be – One. A refusal of 'intercommunion', therefore, diminishes the true character of the Sacrament, makes it represent earth rather than heaven. Our Communion should be a joyful pledge of, and an incitement to, greater visible unity here and now; and the pain should be felt not in the denial of communion to or by our fellow-Christians, but, once again, in the gap between what is to be and what is, between what our Communion reveals and the mess we have actually made of things.

Our Amen at Communion means all sorts of things: it is our greeting, our identification, our pledge to the risen Christ. But above all it is our *response*; for Communion is not something we can create by ourselves, it is available only as the free gift of God. We did not raise Christ from the dead: God did. We, in response to his command, have provided the dry materials for the sacrifice, but it is he who has given us the living Lamb. The Amen is also our word of thanks as we receive back our gifts and our selves, alive with the power and love of the risen Christ.

Nothing in the world is simpler or more obvious than Jesus' great commandments to love; nothing in the world is harder or more potentially depressing. Love God, love your neighbour, love yourself, love your enemy, love one another: oh, yes, if we could only do all these things the Kingdom would come instantly – and with what high hopes we set out to practise them, and how impossible they all turn out to be. Once again the charge of hypocrisy arises: how dare we celebrate this great love feast, when true love is so impossibly beyond our grasp?

As so often, the answer lies hidden in St John's Gospel. His five great chapters on the Last Supper (13—17) are so famous and well loved that we can easily not notice the most surprising thing about them: they don't actually describe the Supper at all. In John there is no 'institution of the Eucharist' as such; perhaps because he assumes his readers will already know the Synoptic account, perhaps because he has already done it in a different way in chapter 6 and is going to do it again, still more originally, in chapter 20. But at the Last Supper itself, Jesus in the other gospel accounts gives us his Body and Blood: what does he give us in John? In the footwashing story,[21] then three more times in so many words,[22] and several more times in other words,[23] and finally also in the prayer of chapter 17, he gives us the 'New Commandment' to love one another.

Instead of a sacrament, a law? Instead of a gift, a demand? It sounds like it at first; yet, on reflection, can we not say that the New Commandment is itself a gift? As Jesus suggests by his language of gift, by the way he acts out the commandment in chapter 13, and by his prayer for the disciples' unity and peace in chapter 17. In the other Gospels, he gives bread and wine: in John's account, his parting gifts are peace[24] and mutual love. Isn't this, in fact, another account of the gift of Communion? For in the gift of his Body and Blood Christ literally *gives us Communion*, that is he gives us peace and love

108

and unity with God, with one another, and with the whole created order. What we could never achieve by ourselves is here being showered upon us. At the Offertory we gave all we could and it was quite inadequate: but now God has taken it, breathed on it, transfigured it, and given it back, and suddenly, miraculously, it *is* enough. We are eating and drinking the only daily bread that truly matters, love itself. John Wesley must have caught this truth when he wrote:

> Our needy souls sustain
>   with fresh supplies of love,
> Till all thy life we gain,
>   and all thy fulness prove,
> And, strengthened by thy perfect grace,
> Behold without a veil thy face.[25]

Love is the gift we receive at the altar: for God, for each other, for the world, and, very importantly, for ourselves. The first essential meaning of our Communion is that *we are beloved*. Without the implanting of that knowledge in our hearts we cannot be the emissaries of love in the world. But when I say Amen, this is what I am daring to believe: that

> Christ loved us, and gave himself over for us,
> an offering and sacrifice to God,
> for the scent of fragrance. (Ephesians 5:1)

And, purified by this love for us, we can respond in kind, as the writer urges us in the same verse:

> So become imitators of God, as beloved children,
> and walk in love . . .

The last phrase reminds us that, finally, there is no distinction between loving and being loved: the one who is loved becomes a lover, the one who loves is beloved. Love is an element in which we are invited to walk, to swim, to breathe. Our Amen is a Yes both to our belovedness and to our vocation to love: we receive Christ, who gave himself as the Bread of the World, and in doing so we also become Christ, the Bread of the World. Even if most of us would find it hard to pray, like St Ignatius before his martyrdom, to be

a meal for the beasts, for it is they who can provide my
    way to God.
I am his wheat, ground fine by the lions' teeth,
to be made purest bread for Christ;[26]

still we are affirming with our Amen that, from now on, our
lives only make sense in a loving, unselfish relationship with
the true and final Body of Christ. Like Jesus, we must be
prepared to be broken and poured out for the world; but with
the faith that, though we often feel drained to the last drop
and beyond, God in his grace can go on filling our cup, like
the widow's cruse, again and again . . .

You prepare a table before me
    in the presence of my enemies;
you anoint my head with oil, my cup overflows.
Surely goodness and mercy shall follow me
all the days of my life;
and I shall dwell in the house of the Lord for ever.[27]

1   2 Corinthians 5:16.
2   John 20:14.
3   Luke 24:15–16.
4   Luke 24:36–37.
5   John 21:4.
6   From 'The Church of God a Kingdom Is' by L. B. Muir-
    head, no. 254 in *Hymns Ancient and Modern Revised*.
7   'The Dream of the Rood', no. 25 in Sweet's *Anglo-Saxon*
    Reader (OUP 1967), 11, 15–23 (my translation).
8   Hebrews 12:18–20.
9   John 10:9.
10 'Catch him if you can', from Clare Matthews' *Alternativity*,
    Chester House Publications 1986.
11 John 20:17.
12 Acts 1:11.
13 See e.g. Luke 24:39, John 20:27; Luke 24:35, John 21:12.
14 1 Corinthians 12:27.
15 Luke 17:20–21.
16 Revelation 3:14.

17 George Herbert, 'Love', from *The Temple* (1633).
18 Rowan Williams, *The Truce of God* (Fount Paperbacks 1983), ch. 2, pp. 28–29.
19 Vincent J. Donovan, *Christianity Rediscovered* (SCM Press 1978), p. 127.
20 Romans 8:33–34.
21 John 13:3–15.
22 John 13:34, 15:12, 15:17.
23 E.g. John 14:15, 21.
24 John 14:27.
25 From 'Author of Life Divine', no. 394 in *Hymns Ancient and Modern Revised*.
26 Ignatius of Antioch, Romans §4, translated by Maxwell Stanforth in *Early Christian Writings*, Penguin 1968.
27 Psalm 23(22):6 (RSV, adapted).

9

Sending
The Dancers Are Elsewhere

It is always pleasant to think, after a time of catastrophe, adventure, or high drama, that everything will be back as it was; the frightening and unfamiliar will give way to the familiar and comforting; normality will return.

But it is rarely so. The drama, the terrors, may be over, but they have left their mark: our adventure has changed us, we are not as we were before, nor can our life be. And often things seem to be worse, as if something were lost: as the animals lost their trust after the Flood,[1] or society its camaraderie after World War II. The traveller may come back home, but he can't settle down:[2] the itch remains in his feet; like Eliot's Magi, who

> . . . returned to our places, these Kingdoms,
> But no longer at ease here, in the old dispensation . . .;[3]

or the Seafarer who sang

> My heart journeys within my breast,
> my mind amid the sea's flood
> journeys wide over the whale's domain,
> the world's corners – it comes to me after,
> fierce and greedy. The lone flier yells,
> whetting my heart along the whale's way,
> irresistibly across the sea's expanse . . .[4]

Did the Prodigal Son ever *really* settle back at home? The gates of Eden are barred with a flaming sword,[5] but it is the

112

sword of our own restless desire: if we did get back in, we would not have it in us to stay.

So with the disciples after Jesus' resurrection. For one brief verse of the gospel account it sounds as if everything really is back to normal: almost comically, after the horrors of Good Friday and the bewilderment of the empty tomb, John tells us that 'they all went back to their own homes'.[6] It is hard for us who have read the next chapter to recapture that first Easter, when they still knew nothing of the ascension or Pentecost. For all they now realized, the events of that Passover weekend had just been a hiccup: Jesus was back, life would carry on as before.

But no: even while appearing to them in bodily form, Jesus would never merely indulge his followers with the sunshine of his rediscovered presence. He was teaching them to let go of him, to see and feel him in a new way, to 'internalize' the relationship. They couldn't hold on to him in their company any more than the authorities could hold him down in the tomb. He was converting them from disciples into apostles, preparing them for their final and irrevocable sending-out in his name. The ascension was a second bereavement, but they had to go through it to receive the 'second blessing' of Pentecost. 'Don't be amazed, but *go*,' says the angel to the women;[7] 'don't cling on to me, *go*,' says Jesus to Mary Magdalene;[8] and in every one of the farewell stories[9] there is this same refusal of cosiness, this insistence that from now on they, the disciples, are to play his part: 'as the Father has sent me, even so I send you';[10] 'you shall be my witnesses'.[11]

And, as Acts and Paul make clear, this was understood in a radical sense: they had not just been commissioned as Jesus' deputies or delegates, but as his very Body, filled with his very Holy Spirit. When the angel in Acts chapter 1 says that 'this Jesus who has been taken up from you into heaven will come in just the way you have seen him going into heaven',[12] could we be meant to understand, not some remote 'second coming', but the events of the next chapter, Pentecost? The second coming of Jesus was at the baptism of the Body of Christ with the Holy Spirit. As he poured out his life on the cross, so now, with the same unstinting generosity, he pours

113

out the Spirit which he received on our behalf at his baptism. From now on the disciples would not be going out with Christ or for Christ, but in Christ and *as Christ*. The Upper Room was to be left behind like a slough; the sphere of operations was the world itself. The true mission was beginning.

The giving of the Spirit is the whole point of the gospel story, which without it would remain a perplexing if edifying tale, of no enduring importance. The Gospels are only gospel because they open out into the present, finishing with an invitation or challenge to the reader, like those in Jesus' own stories: Christ ended up by pouring out his Spirit on his people, and in the light of that same Spirit this story is now being written; and it is the same Spirit who confronts every reader of it – now you can come into the story, take the plunge into the picture, be part of the next episode yourself.[13]

And the final sending out is the whole point of the Eucharist: so much so that its most popular name, curiously shunned by many who are in the forefront of Christian mission, is the Mass, *missa*, the sending. The 'concluding rite' or 'dis*miss*al', with which it ends, is not merely (as it sometimes seems) a convenient way to round it all off neatly: it is essential and integral, the com*miss*ioning of Christ's people to go and be Christ in and for the world, to lose themselves for his sake and the gospel's. So we pray, in the Anglican liturgy, that God will make us a living sacrifice to his praise and glory.

The end of the Communion is a moment of intimacy, peace and great gladness, as we celebrate our unity with Christ and with all his people. A silence just after Communion can be a time of warmth and peace and timelessness. It is good to be there, leaning on the Lord's breast, trusting and praying. But, during the silence, the Lord moves on. The vessels are cleared, the altar left empty. The silence is broken, and back we all go to our homes . . .

There is a sense in which we rightly take with us that moment of silence and holiness; as the disciples can never have forgotten their good times with Jesus. But there is also an *improper* desire to cling on to what is here, to try and stay with the bodily Jesus, to refuse to move out into the chilly world. We cannot, of course, physically remain in church once the dismissal is given: but it is all too possible to remain at this stage inside ourselves, even to take it with us into the world, not noticing that the communion fire has become a churchy cosiness.

For when we are told to *go out*, it means more than going out from the service and the building. It means – as it meant for the Apostles – going out from the safeness of the Church into the dangerousness of the world; from the security of a nice Christian surrounding into the great secular insecurity that surrounds us, where everything will be questioned and nothing taken for granted. And we can, if we like, protect ourselves from that world by remaining in a sort of Christian bubble, filling our lives with church-centred activity, continually reassuring ourselves of the impregnability of our faith; but that will not be mission. We can, indeed, make ourselves look very missionary by going all out to serve others or bring them to Christ, but, if it is all done from within the bubble and for the sake of the bubble (and 'always to be talking about Jesus' can be an excellent way of insulating ourselves, as well of driving those around us to drink), it is not true mission. Mission means going right out from the physical and spiritual upper room, into the world where no holds are barred.

What, then, is meant by the 'eucharistic life'? It doesn't mean going to church every five minutes, and it doesn't mean walling oneself in with Christian thoughts and Christian friends, important though these are. Rather, it means reproducing in everyday life the pattern of the Eucharist, which is the pattern of Christ: living a life to which penitence and forgiveness are integral; open to the glory of God in even the most unexpected settings; listening for his Word in whatever is said, and in the spaces between; testing one's belief against the belief and the unbelief of the world; offering oneself for others, and others to God; entering into the darkness, brokenness and bloodiness of things in the nakedness of unprotected faith; and enjoying to the full our communion, our community with people of every possible kind, and with the whole created order. We pray God to make us a living sacrifice, but by itself that's too narrow and negative: we must become, in fact, a living sac*rament*, giving with love and receiving with thanks.

Such a life could not be artificially engineered ('now how am I going to integrate penitence into my meeting with Ken this morning? . . . and did I really rejoice in my communion with Auntie's poodle last Monday?'); and it could never be more than partially realized. But it *will* be partly realized if we let the words and actions of the Eucharist sink into our souls; and through that regular and costly prayer which keeps our life open to the dimension of God and the reality of his Kingdom, and imperceptibly converts our whole life into an act of prayer and praise. Our real response to the Word of the Lord, and to the gift of his Body and Blood, is not a piously muttered (or earnestly shouted) formula: our true Amen, beginning from that moment, is the life we live.

Probably the profoundest biblical meditation on this theme is Paul's great passage on the apostolic life in his second letter to the Corinthians, particularly from 1:1 to 6:13. Throughout this section he is depicting the Christian apostle as a vessel, empty of self-concern and so available for God. If we suffer, we will be the means of consolation to others;[14] if we boast, it can only be of what God has done through us;[15] if we come close to God, it is to reflect his glory (perhaps without feeling it ourselves) upon those around us:[16]

. . . for it is not ourselves that we proclaim,
but Christ Jesus, the Lord,
and ourselves, your servants through Jesus.
For it is God, who says 'out of darkness light will shine',
who has shone in our hearts,
for the lighting of the knowledge of the glory of God
in the face of Christ.
And we have this treasure in vessels of earthenware,
so that the overflowing of power
may be of God and not from us.
In everything we are hard pressed, but not hemmed in;
perplexed, but not despairing;
persecuted, but not abandoned;

struck down, but not destroyed;
always carrying the deadness of Jesus around in our body,
so that the life of Jesus too may be manifested in our body.
For we, the living ones, are always being handed over to
    death on account of Jesus,
so that the life of Jesus, too, may be manifested in our
    mortal flesh.
Thus death is at work in us, life in you.[17]

At the Eucharist and in our prayers we offer ourselves as
vessels, chalices, for the light, life and glory of God; ready for
breaking (and the word for 'earthen' in this passage is derived
from the Greek *ostrakon*, which means a bit of *broken* pottery),
and ready for pouring out, like the woman's alabaster jar,[18]
at the feet of Christ.

All of which may sound solemn and unenjoyable: indeed,
Paul's devoutest admirer might not suppose his company was
always the greatest of fun. But what he describes here is not
nearly as unattractive as it may seem; for the empty vessel
will always be receptive to what is around, sitting lightly to
the things that weigh most of us down so much. Straitlaced
gloominess is a feature of self-love and self-concern, while the
life of self-giving and self-offering, which Paul describes, will
almost by definition have a huge capacity for enjoyment.
Once again, it is the meek who inherit the earth.

'I may say this watch is mine,' said Metropolitan Anthony
once, enclosing a great pocket-watch in his fist; 'I may have
gained a watch, but I have lost a hand.' We are to be an
open-handed people, enjoying our earth in a way those full
up with possessing it never can: now it is our turn to give
and receive hospitality as Jesus did.

And our enjoyment, our celebration, if it is to be truly missionary, must also not be safely contained within the Christian
bubble. In a sense it is true that we are to be living sacraments: but it is also true, as the Quakers have long been
aware, that we must learn to discover the whole world as the
sacrament of God's love. There is forgiveness, and glory,
and the Word of Truth, and faith, and self-offering, and

brokenness, and consecration, and communion, way beyond the boundaries of the visible Church: and if we are really beginning to reproduce the pattern of those things in our own lives, we shall not be threatened when we find the same dance elsewhere; unlike the writers of the 13th Article of Religion of the Church of England, who believed that

> works done before the grace of Christ,
> and the inspiration of his Spirit,
> are not pleasant to God . . .
> we doubt not but they have the nature of sin;

or the disciples who told Jesus they

> 'saw someone throwing out demons in your name,
> and we tried to stop him, because he wasn't coming along with us.'
> But Jesus said, 'Don't stop him:
> for whoever is not against you is on your side.'[19]

In parts of the West Indian Church there rages a controversy about the celebration of carnival. The carnival always involves a lot of drunkenness, licentiousness, carousing, and probably most of the other things Paul mentions in his formidable list of the 'works of the flesh';[20] so, argue one group, Christians should keep away from it, and find instead a more 'wholesome' recreation for the day – and off they all go for an exceedingly wholesome picnic at the other end of the island. Not so, say the other group: the carnival may *involve* bad behaviour, but that doesn't make it a bad event; there is no harm in our being there and enjoying ourselves and, who knows? even setting a good example.

But the good example isn't the point. Even the prospect of a 'wholesome picnic' is preferable to the sinister idea that Christians *should* indeed be getting involved with the world, but only with an ulterior motive – proselytizing, or moral reform, or some other version of getting others into our bubble: as Christians are sometimes encouraged to make friends with non-Christians, not for a much-needed spiritual breather, but *in order to get them in*. This (it is argued) is why Jesus spent so much time in disreputable company – he was out to get them and make them Christian, and, presumably, respectable.

If that had been the case, the religious establishment would have had no interest in having him crucified, for they would have recognized in him an undercover agent for their own cause of religious respectability. Whereas, in fact, there is no evidence that Jesus did, or ever wanted to, make anyone respectable. The healing which he brought to this sinful, recognizably sick section of society was not a passport to respectability or decency or success or positive thinking or even the pearly gates; it was simply the glorious but absolutely shocking message that God loved and cared for them as they were. To put it another way, these people were regarded as being beyond every possible social and religious pale; Jesus didn't show them how to get back across the pale, rather he proclaimed that God's love knows no pales, that as far as he was concerned the pale didn't exist, that people were every bit as precious and important to God one side of it as the other – even that, inasmuch as there was a pale, it was the self-styled 'righteous' who were creating it and putting themselves on the wrong side of it. Here indeed was matter for crucifixion.[21]

So it is always worrying if the main effect of Christian mission is to make people tame and well behaved. Of course it is wonderful that the Gospel can save people from slavery to drink, drugs, or depersonalized sex; but it can also save them from slavery to wealth and power (whether their own or other people's), from unquestioning obedience to the authorities, and from general complacency – a far less comfortable conversion. We read in Acts how the newly converted Christians 'found favour with the whole people';[22] but it was a different story once the Gospel began to threaten the established religion or the local economy.[23]

In any case, we cannot manipulate the Holy Spirit; we cannot know the purpose of our engagement with the world, or engineer its outcome. We can only try to keep up with Christ's amazing and highly offbeat dance through the most unexpected quarters of the world; to listen for God's tune and sing along with it, for no other purpose than the sheer joy of singing. By doing so we may well become unwittingly available for his purposes; like Robert Browning's Pippa, who changed everyone's lives just by singing outside their windows.[24] As with our own salvation, so with other people's: it is only when we lose all interest in it that we will stand any chance of bringing it about. The vessels must always be empty.

This attitude to 'mission' is powerfully expressed by Irene Claremont de Castillejo in a chapter on 'The Rainmaker Ideal'. She tells the story of a Chinese village desperate for rain:

> In despair they sent far afield for a 'Rainmaker'. When the little old man arrived, they asked him what he needed to effect his magic and he replied, 'Nothing, only a quiet place where I can be alone.' They gave him a little house and there he lived quietly doing the things one has to do in life, and on the third day the rain came . . .
>
> If only we could be rainmakers! I am not of course thinking literally of rain. I am thinking of those people . . . who go about their ordinary business with no fuss, not ostensibly helping others, not giving advice, not continually or self-consciously praying for guidance or striving for mystical union with God, not even especially noticeable, yet around whom things happen.
>
> Others seem to live more fully for their presence: possibilities of work appear unexpectedly or people offer their services unsought, houses fall vacant for the homeless, lovers meet. Life blossoms all around them without their lifting a finger and, as likely as not, without anyone attributing to them any credit for the happenings, least of all themselves . . .
>
> We have forgotten how to allow. The essence of the Rainmaker is that he knows how to allow. The Rainmaker walks in the middle of the road, neither held back by the past nor hurrying towards the future, neither lured to the right nor to the left, but allowing the past and the future, the outer world of the right and the inner images of the left

120

all to play upon him while he attends, no more than attends, to the living moment in which these forces meet.[25]

To hear and follow the beat of Christ's often distant dance, we must be content, like the Rainmaker, to attend; ridding ourselves of the propensity to finish people's sentences for them, and also to finish God's sentences for him. We need to hear what is *really* being said, not what we are predisposed to hear ('and how are *you* today?' – 'terrible, Father.' – 'fine, good, goodbye . . . and now how are *you*? . . .'); and we need to hear what is in the gaps and the silences and the hesitations too. Jesus 'knew what was in Man',[26] but his uncanny ability to see what was really the matter didn't stem from any supernatural extra features God had endowed him with, a spiritual bionic ear; but from a deep and loving attentiveness to people and the world and God, which enabled him to see and hear what was really going on. Anyone can tell when there's something the matter with someone else if they set their mind to it; but mostly we prefer not to.

Attentiveness to God, in sustained prayer, must be at the heart of our attentiveness to the melody and harmony of his world and his people. Times of being alone, of attuning ourselves to the sound of his silence, are a necessity. But they are very difficult. It is hard to make such times in our lives, easy to make excuses, easy to make time for almost anything else except the one thing which is really needed. Mary chose the better part,[27] and it was *not* an easy option.

For how hard it is, even when we do manage to elbow out a time for prayer, to get really still, to feel any communion with God. People are always referring to the old man who said to the Curé d'Ars, 'I look at [God], and he looks at me, and we're happy' – but it isn't that easy. An ever-increasing number of books tell you how simple it is to be still and contemplate, and they are all most convincing while you read them, and prayer seems just as hard again once you have laid them down. The racing thoughts continue to race, the body continues to itch, the all-pervading rhythm of breathing and mantra and heartbeat just doesn't pervade, however dim the light and however many icons one contemplates and however authentic one's bodily position. Such, at least, is my experience, and I suspect that, like most secret shameful personal experiences, I share it with many others. No doubt there really are those who regularly achieve a deep ethereal stillness of mind and soul, but they are probably less than the literature would have us believe; and this needs pointing out to save the rest of us from feeling like spiritual misfits because we aren't born contemplatives.

Nevertheless, it is also my experience that, somewhere underneath the confusing jumble which passes for a time of prayer, there really *does* lie the pearl of great price, and that it is, therefore, in spite of everything, a necessary and worthwhile endeavour. Indeed, if prayer were all smooth and easy and beautiful, if it was what we spend all our day just longing to do, it would be highly suspect, because it would be so out of character with the rest of Christian experience. It is, in fact, a hard, mundane and frustrating activity; but, like our humanity itself which has much the same characteristics, it can be the vehicle of God's glory. Good things, and also uncomfortable but essential things, do come to the surface during prayer; and prayer does make a difference to life, because life just doesn't make so much sense without it. The aim must always be to break down the barriers between prayer and life, to endue life with a contemplative and attentive spirit, to transform life into one great act of prayer: but that is unlikely to happen without those definite and awkward times being set aside.

And, when it all becomes too unbearable, it is helpful and important to remember that this prayer is not something I am doing for my own sake, to get me right with God, or to make me feel good, or to integrate my personality – though it will sometimes have those effects, and very excellent too – but as part of the Body to which I belong and to which I am committed: a Body, furthermore, which (however much it feels like a 'mighty tortoise'[28]) is on the move, has been sent out to discover, to celebrate and to be part of Christ's work in the world. My prayer is part of that; however alone and hopeless it may feel, it is in fact contributing to, and supported by, the mission and the prayer of the whole people of God.

The world, like the epileptic boy,[29] needs our prayer for its healing.

That is a good thing to remember when praying alone; by the same token it can often be easier to pray with others, even if in silence. It can be good to ask for the prayers of others; of friends, of religious communities who exist to make this contribution to the Body of the Church; and of the saints. And it can be very good to pray before the Reserved Sacrament in church, a sign of the eternally incarnate and vulnerable Christ, and a perpetual reminder of the Eucharist which sums up his life and our participation in it, and from which we have been sent out on his mission.

The title of this book is ambiguous. In John's Gospel Jesus describes himself as the Bread of Life, and at the Eucharist we are fed with his freshness, for our own sake and as priests of the world. We are sent out, in our turn, as bread for the world. But the world is also the subject of our Liturgy; the vehicle of God's glory, the source of his Word. It is the world itself we offer for consecration; the world we revere, in all its brokenness, as the Body of Christ. In the fragility of the eucharistic bread we perceive the fragile world; and we go out towards the world in the same spirit of reverence and awe with which we approached the Sacrament; for the world, too, is sacrament, the precious bread of God's life.

Finally, we are bidden to go *in peace*. The spirit of peace which underlies the whole Liturgy, in songs and greetings, biddings and blessings, is the spirit with which we are now charged: not as a protective bubble but as the motive of our going. The spirit of reverence in which we held up the host is the spirit in which we now hold the world, as God showed it to Julian of Norwich,

> a little thing, the size of a hazel-nut, on the palm of my hand, round like a ball. I looked at it thoughtfully and wondered, 'What is this?' And the answer came, 'It is all that is made.' I marvelled that it continued to exist and did not disintegrate; it was so small. And again my mind

supplied the answer, 'It exists, both now and for ever, because God loves it.'[30]

That small fragile thing, the Bread of the World, is in our hands: as the world's priest we offered it, as the world's priest we received it, and as the world's priest we now walk into its holy ground, shod not with heavy trampling boots but only with the 'equipment of the Gospel of peace':[31] celebrants of God's peace and love, singers of his glory.

In practice this will lead us into many hard places: if not (like the saints in Hebrews 11) to being stoned and sawn in two and to going about in the skins of sheep and goats, then certainly, sooner or later, to acts of sacrificial generosity, to intractable moral dilemmas, to derision or persecution, or, perhaps worse still, to the darkness of self-doubt. But this is also the narrow pilgrim way to heaven; heaven which is not a celestial seaside resort, but the full knowledge of what we now only darkly glimpse,[32] the final assumption of our true name[33] and stature[34] as God's children, of our unique and proper place in the Body of Christ: a place which can only be gained by losing all interest in status whether earthly or heavenly; by plunging into the waters of life; by enjoying with Christ the feast of that life, to the full.

1 See Genesis 9:2; or, for a fuller account, *The Log of the Ark* by Kenneth Walker and Geoffrey Boumphrey.
2 Like Frodo in Tolkein's *Lord of the Rings*, Book VI, ch. 9.
3 T. S. Eliot, *The Journey of the Magi*.
4 'The Seafarer', no. 27 in Sweet's *Anglo-Saxon Reader*, 11, 58–64 (my translation).
5 Genesis 3:24.
6 John 20:10.
7 Mark 16:6–7.
8 John 20:17.
9 Matthew 28:16ff., Luke 24:44ff., John 20:19ff., John 21:15ff., Mark 16:15ff., Acts 1:4ff.
10 John 20:21.
11 Acts 1:8.

12   Acts 1:11.
13   See, classically, John 20:31.
14   2 Corinthians 1:3–7.
15   2 Corinthians 1:12–14.
16   2 Corinthians 3:7–18.
17   2 Corinthians 4:5–12.
18   Mark 14:3.
19   Luke 9:49–50.
20   Galatians 5:19–21.
21   See e.g. Luke 5:32, 15:7. Repentance didn't have quite such respectable overtones in those days.
22   Acts 2:47.
23   See e.g. Acts 19:23–end, Acts 21:27–28.
24   Robert Browning, 'Pippa Passes', *Poetical Works of Robert Browning*, vol. 3, Clarendon Press 1988.
25   Irene Claremont de Castillejo, *Knowing Woman* (Harper and Row 1974), ch. 9; and cf. Hermann Hesse's description of the Rainmaker in 'The Three Lives' at the end of *The Glass Bead Game*.
26   John 2:25.
27   Luke 10:42.
28   This refers to the verse (I'm not sure where it comes from):
     Like a mighty tortoise moves the Church of God:
     Brothers, we are treading where we've always trod.
29   Mark 9:29.
30   Julian of Norwich, *Revelations of Divine Love*, trans. Clifton Wolters (Penguin 1966), ch. 5.
31   Ephesians 6:15.
32   1 Corinthians 13:12.
33   See Revelation 2:17.
34   Ephesians 4:13.

Appendix

A Hymn

(Written for Dudley J. Hill's tune 'Leeds', no. 207 in the
Mirfield Mission Hymn Book)

Lord, who once victorious through the waters came;
    Lord, who once baptized us that your Church might
       grow:
Call us now from dryness through the depths of love,
    So through us may streams of living water flow.

Lord, you healed the sin of those who turned to you;
    Still your absolution as your Church we find:
Heal the hurts among us, so at one may we
    Pour forgiveness on the guilt of all mankind.

Peace you gave your people on the night you died;
    Peace we share and with a holy kiss we seal:
Filled with peace beyond the knowledge of this world
    Grant that dear world's wounds together we may heal.

Then you shared your very self as bread and wine,
    Dying for Communion in that evening hour:
May we live this same Communion day by day,
    And through us be known your reconciling power.

Then you came as Spirit on your praying Church;
    Hands were laid, and members knew their ministry:
Lord, confirm our Confirmation – may we all
    Go in peace to serve the world and set it free.

Young and old, and black and white, and high and low,
Dead and living, bad and good, and rich and poor,
All and one you loved us: so may one and all
Live your praise throughout your world for evermore.

A Eucharistic Prayer

Father, all-powerful and everliving God,
again and again we give you thanks and praise
for the wonder of creation, the joy of life, and the hope of
eternal glory.

We praise you for our universe, for the unimaginable depths
of time and space;
for all we have discovered, and for all that is still beyond our
imagining.

We praise you for our planet, in its richness and its fragility,
and for the abundance of life in all its forms.

We praise you for making us in your own image;
for sharing with us your work of creation;
and for your overflowing delight in all that is made.

And so, with the whole of our being,
we join with your angels and archangels,
with all the powers of heaven and earth,
and with all your faithful people in every age,
in their timeless song of wonder and praise:

holy, Holy,   holy,
Lord, God of hosts:
Heaven and earth are full of your glory:
Hosanna in the highest.

Blessed is he who comes in the name of the Lord:
Hosanna in the highest.

Father, in your creative love you call us to become your
children,

the inheritors of your Kingdom and its glory:
but again and again we have turned from your calling
to the paths of idolatry and destruction.

You have invited us back to our true life
through the witness of your prophets and saints in many
    times and cultures;
and, in the fullness of time, you gave us your Son,
born of a woman and crowned with your Holy Spirit.
In his life and in his death
he opened wide the gates of your Kingdom;
and, when you had raised him from the dead,
he poured out your Spirit on all who would receive it,
anointing them as your children with the promise of your
    glorious freedom.

And so, Father, we ask you now
to send that same Holy Spirit upon us and upon our offerings,
to consecrate us afresh for your service in the Body of Christ,
and to make holy these gifts of bread and wine
which we offer in the name of all humanity,
the name of Jesus Christ.

Who, on the night he was betrayed,
having loved his brothers and sisters in your world,
showed now the full extent of that love.

He took bread, gave you thanks, broke the bread,
and shared it with his disciples, saying:
Take this, all of you, and eat it:
This is my body, given for you.

In the same way, after supper, he took the cup, filled with
    wine.
He gave you thanks, and shared it with his disciples, saying:
Take this, all of you, and drink from it:
This is my blood, poured out for you,
a new covenant of forgiveness and hope.
Whenever you drink it, you will live my life afresh.

Great is the mystery of our faith:

Christ has died;
Christ has risen;
Christ lives in us now.

And so, Father, as we enter again into the mystery
of the suffering and death of your Son Jesus Christ;
as we celebrate his mighty resurrection
and his victorious procession through the depths and the
    heights:
we offer you this bread and this cup,
the saving sign of his sacrifice and ours.

As we eat and drink these holy gifts
in anticipation of your heavenly banquet,
unite us in communion with him, and with all your people
across the world and down the ages;
with your servant Pope *N*, with our bishops *N* and *N*,
with our fellow-Christians, and all who serve you with a
    sincere heart;
with blessed Mary, with your apostles and prophets,
with all who have witnessed to your Kingdom by their lives
    and by their deaths,
and with those suffering now for your truth and your justice.

May this Holy Communion be a living reality, in us and in
    our world;
break down the barriers of war, selfishness, and oppression;
bring an end to exploitation and prejudice,
and renew the integrity of your creation.
Wherever there is brokenness and despair, bring healing and
    hope,
and life in the shadows of death.

Inspire us and your whole Church with the courage and the
    vision
to be the living signs, in this broken world,
of your Gospel of peace and new life.

Our prayer, our selves, and our lives
we offer you, Father, in the name of your Son Jesus Christ,

by whom, with whom, and in whom, in the unity of the Holy
  Spirit,
all honour and glory be yours
from all your people and from the whole of creation,
now and always and through the ages of ages.

Amen